CREWE and its PEOPLE

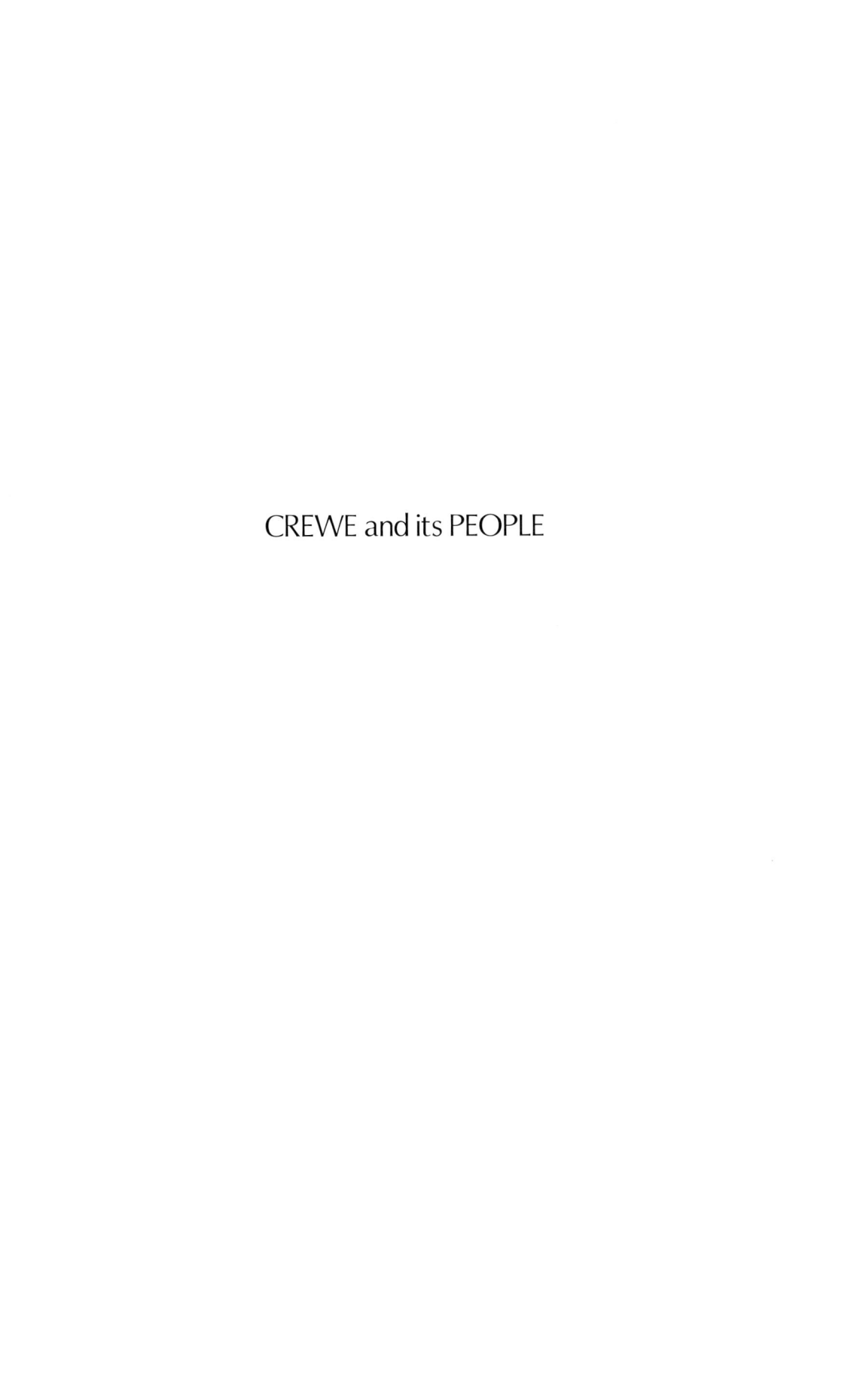

Copyright © Jules Hornbrook
ISBN 978-0-9538877-2-9
Published in the United Kingdom
by MPire books of Crewe 2009

All rights reserved. This publication may not be reproduced, stored in a retrieval system, or transmitted, in any form or by any means electronic, mechanical, photocopying, recording or otherwise, without the prior permission of the publishers. Every effort has been made to contact present copyright owners to any photographs that appear in this book which are not properly credited. We will do our utmost to include any acknowledgments to all parties and amend any errors or facts that are not correct, in subsequent reprints of this book.

CREWE and its PEOPLE

Jules Hornbrook

In memory of
May Howard

Contents

Peter Andrews	*Only Fools and Horses*	*007*
Rob Allen	*West End Boy*	*011*
Christine Messam	*The Jamaica Inn*	*015*
Shanaze Reade	*Top of the World*	*019*
Diane Dyer	*Growing the Family Tree*	*023*
Toby Robinson	*Jack of all Trades*	*027*
Nick Bayes	*Tower Struck Down*	*031*
Brian Silvester	*A Life in Politics*	*035*
May Howard	*Queen of the Washers*	*039*
Andy Gilbert	*Thin Blue Lines*	*043*
Nadia Dawson	*On the Buses*	*047*
Mike Ramm	*Making 'em Laugh*	*051*
Gary Delaney	*The Railroaders*	*055*
Kevin Street	*Teaching the Game*	*059*
Ed Whitby	*Made in Crewe*	*063*
Dorothy Flude	*A Social Conscience*	*067*
Andy Scoffin	*Painting the Town Red*	*071*
Jo Hassan	*Keeping the Faith*	*075*
John Rhodes	*United We Stand*	*079*
Tim Prevett	*The Ghost Whisperer*	*083*
Elaine Dodd	*Building Bridges in Town*	*087*
Bill Andrew	*Life on the Footplate*	*091*
Peter Kent	*Flying the Red Flag*	*095*
Wendy Hadaway	*Dorothy's Red Shoes*	*099*
Mark Potts	*Remembering the Fallen*	*103*
David Thomas	*The Green Shoots of Hope*	*107*
Rob Wykes	*The Power of Three*	*111*
Marco Criscuolo	*Watching the Cattle Market*	*115*
Howard Curran	*Time Gentlemen, Please...*	*119*
Ray Bispham	*Into the Limelight*	*123*
John Fleet	*Mr Crewe Alexandra*	*127*
Paul Ancell	*The Council Guy*	*131*
Glynne Henshall	*Preserving the Railway Heritage*	*135*
Dave Preece	*A Potted History*	*139*
Chris Turner	*King for a Season*	*143*
Matt Owen	*The Wonder of Crewe*	*147*
David Cope	*Mill Street Marbles*	*151*
Peter Ollerhead	*Grumpy Old Men*	*155*
Albert Dean	*Voice of the Airwaves*	*159*
Joey Singleton	*Punches and Pints*	*163*

Foreword

There have been many history books written about Crewe, whilst others have told a story through images alone. So I set out to explore the people and, hopefully, weave a tale of the town by exploring forty lives that highlight some of the many idiosyncrasies that make Crewe unique. It's a lucky dip of characters - some prominent and easily recognised, others relative unknowns who go about their business with little fuss or desire to be noticed. Everyone has a story and this book, I hope, paints a picture of modern-day Crewe through the eyes of those who have lived, worked and played there...

Acknowledgments

To all of the people who agreed to be interviewed, it has been a pleasure coaxing stories from many of you who thought that there was nothing to tell. On a practical note, Mark Potts and Tony Marks from Mpire Books of Crewe have been a joy to work with. Additional photos have come from Simon J. Newbury, Mat Hall, Howard Curran, John Yuill, Cliff Gallimore, Dave Shepherd, Mission Sports Management and R. A. Cade, plus many from the personal collections of those who feature within the book. Finally, thanks must go to the many friends and family who have poured over the text as it emerged, checking details and giving me some great feedback. Thanks all.

Peter Andrews
Only Fools and Horses

Born and bred in Crewe, Peter Andrews has never lived more than ten minutes walk from the town centre. Associated with bustling markets, stallholders and in particular, the fresh meat trade from a young age, when an opportunity to join the market management team arose he didn't have to think twice. He was made for the role.

"I first came to the market as a kid, shopping with mum. I loved the noise, colour and the smells, and that so many people were chatting and laughing. It was a real social occasion. So it was no surprise that I got my first job helping out on one of the meat counters. Back then there was a full row of butchers inside the hall and it was a very competitive environment. There was plenty of shouting and banter as traders tried to get the customers to their stalls. I worked for Davis & Sons, and Andrews' Butchers (not related) was nearby. The old guy on their stand - who looked about 90 years old - would fall asleep with a cigarette in his mouth while he stood at the counter. I'd try and convince customers that he was dead and that they should come to us!"

Butchery was Peter's chosen career, and after college he stayed within the industry as a meat and poultry inspector. Spells with other council departments followed, but joining the market team was an obvious progression in the 1990s. Across the decades he's seen more change than most. "The layout was different when I was a kid, and there were tin stalls outside - in fact, most of the outdoor structures have now been remodelled. The old Co-op and its car park were next door and there were two white lines that ran across the market and defined the boundary, their right of way if you like. The manager came out each day to check that the traders weren't crossing the line. So some did just that to wind him up!"

Humour has always played a big part in market life with laughter and practical jokes essential in keeping morale high. "April Fools, and in particular, toilet gags are always popular. One year, the council posted some new regulations up on the main notice board. We adapted one and told the traders that they must bring their own toilet rolls to work. They fell for it. So next year we changed the opening times, pretending that traders could only use them alternate half hours! We were rolling about laughing, but they always get us back."

Perhaps it's the camaraderie that keeps the market folk together, despite many challenges over the years. "When the covered Market Centre opened nearby it was full of big-name shops and looked great, but we knew that it would never have the same character as the stalls and old hall. They even rebuilt the front of the theatre but people liked the personal touch that some of the older businesses offered, like the cake shop that used to be on the corner of the square. You could talk and swap stories about market life with the friendly staff. They knew all of the traders and you felt part of a big family. The cake shop, restaurant and market toilets were all huddled together,

and we also had some storage space on the first floor above the box office that sold tickets for the shows. It was chaotic, but there was a great feeling about the place. Even the outdoor stalls were tightly packed together, and if it rained you could walk right through the market without getting wet by dodging under the canopies."

Jostling for trading space and customers, stallholders have always fallen out. However, while many sections of society have become increasingly fragmented Peter believes that the Crewe market community has become closer in recent times. "There's always been plenty of rivalry around the stalls and numerous disputes have taken place. After certain incidents they wouldn't speak to each other for weeks. There was a desire to be the best and to make their business succeed. They didn't want to give each other the edge and they'd argue about an inch of space, the size of advertising boards and who had the most light! Years ago I did a warden's job, covering some of the really tough Crewe neighbourhoods, but it was nothing compared to some of the arguments I saw on the market. They'd shout, push and shove and sometimes cause a scene to keep customers away from a rival stall. But they rarely came to blows. Things are definitely more chilled out these days. They help each other. You can leave a fellow trader looking after your stall, just as people once left their back doors open. I'd like to think that we help the situation by spreading the stalls evenly and trying to make sure that any newcomers don't upset the happy balance that exists."

Maintaining that equilibrium has never been easy, as multiple traders often want to cash in on current trends. The goods sold across the stalls have changed regularly as fashions and crazes come and go. "In the 1980s there were eight or nine material stores selling a fantastic range of fabrics in hundreds of wonderful colours, but now there's just one or two. People buy on-line and at the bigger discount shops and this has hit some of the traders hard. I remember when unisex sweatshirts became popular and every stall tried to sell them, especially the ones adorned in trendy logos and slogans. They all wanted a slice of the action and it caused friction. We were out almost every day making sure things didn't get nasty. When it's your livelihood tempers can flare if someone steps on your patch. Ultimately, they had to get on with it and deal with the competition. We just kept the peace."

Daily disputes are not always down to the traders, as the Crewe market area sits on a council-run car park. "Somebody from the council came over to me one day and said that his car had been scratched by a trader. Unfortunately, he'd parked his car in the square on market day. That means that it's not a car park until the market has gone. So I asked him if he thought that it was a market or a car park. He could sense that I was testing him so he kept quiet. I explained that if it was a market he shouldn't have been parked there, and if it was a car park he'd parked there at his own risk. He walked off in a huff!"

There have been light-hearted moments too, like nearly delaying a Lyceum Theatre production. "We'd had a market running and we weren't quite ready to release the square for car parking. One woman asked when she would be allowed on, and I told her that it wouldn't be long. Then she asked again ten minutes later, looking a little concerned. I hadn't realised that it was the lead actress from a show that evening and that she had an hour's make-up to go through!"

So what does the future hold? "The market will survive, because people will want it to survive. It's like steam trains - they stopped building them but people still want to ride on them. Saturdays are busy because traders can have a job and still run a stall at the weekend. We have also seen more of the Polish people shopping here, as they seem to love the market. So I remain positive. The best bit about the job is the people. Recessions come and go, buildings change and new fads are always popping up. But the people will ensure that markets are always popular…"

Peter with Del Boy lookalike Maurice Canham.

Rob Allen
West End Boy

Before the arrival of Leighton Hospital in the late 1960s, like most Crewe kids, Rob Allen was born at the Barony Hospital in Nantwich. The quaint market town would not, however, be the setting for his childhood years. Instead, the youngster would grow up in a dysfunctional but close-knit family around Crewe's West End...

"As a young kid we lived on Totty's Hall, before they built the Leighton Park estate. It was a pre-war house on Wheelman Road, nothing special but home to our family. I had what many people would now call a cosmopolitan childhood that must have looked odd to those who didn't know us. My mum came to Crewe from Ireland to work on the railways, and my dad followed some time later. They had three girls before I was born, but they split up while I was still a baby. Mum met a Jamaican man, so there was an Irish woman, a young ginger-haired kid and a black man! It sounds like a joke, but that's how it was. It gets more complicated; my sisters lived with my biological dad in a house just around the corner. That was unusual for the time - a single man, working full-time, struggling to bring up three girls on his own! Then my mother and step dad had another baby, my brother, who was half-caste. So I grew up in a wonderfully multi-cultural environment."

A complicated set-up, but surely the problems were the same as we see today around fragmented estates? "Without putting rose-tinted specs on, I remember a real sense of community back then. It was a mix, and I'm sure it would make a great case for sociologists today. And yet people accepted each other for what and who they were. There were incidents, and my step dad told me how it was when he first came to the town. There was hatred towards blacks and Irish and that is something that has stayed with me. There was blatant racism, here in Crewe.

Fireworks were pushed through doors, but that wasn't acceptable. By that I mean the heads of households, not the police, would soon stamp out any trouble. They were the power holders and keeping order was in their interests. It didn't happen again! Times were hard and money was tight, but most people were working and that made a difference. I remember neighbours coming home from Crewe Works, Rolls-Royce and also the factories in Sandbach - Fodens and ERF. So minds were occupied and there was no reason to hate. That seems to have changed across recent decades and what worries me today is how migrant workers are targeted and accused of taking jobs when times are hard. I see a lot of similarities between the 1960s and the early part of the 21st century when many Eastern European migrant workers arrived in Crewe. Suddenly, when life gets tough, there's animosity towards these people. So whenever I get a sniff of racism it infuriates me. My experience of living and growing up with immigrants is that they are incredibly hard working, principled people. They had the courage to come to a foreign country and rebuild a life in Crewe. I think that's amazing."

Smith Grove street party, 1977.

For some years it was Rob who dodged jibes from other kids as he entered the Crewe school system, but missing class was also on his agenda. "I think psychiatrists would suggest that someone with my background would have identity issues. I was teased and taunted, especially when my black dad collected my half-caste brother and me from Totty's Hall School. But your true mates see through colour and complicated families. At school I dealt with things but often found ways to stay at home, maybe because I had a problem with the system. So I got a tag, labelled a difficult lad. When I was seven they sent me to an approved school on the Wirral - like a local authority care home - for just over a year. The place was full of older lads from Manchester and Liverpool. So I had to learn a lot - and quickly. When I came back to Crewe I was very subdued. I suppose it worked because I hardly missed another day of school. I didn't want to be taken away again. Today, more questions would be asked. But it happened and it was a life-changing experience. It was like joining the Army - I just did it early in life."

The family unit moved a few hundred yards to Smith Grove and that was home right through to the end of Rob's senior school days. "They gave me a learning mentor when I returned from care and that was the catalyst for me. I discovered books, learning and a way ahead. It sounds quite romantic but that's the power of education. The next step was senior school, and I was part of the first intake of boys at Kings Grove. They'd merged Kingsway and the old girls grammar school, so it was a special time. We'd sneak into the 6th form common room in the late 70s and see punk and pop posters on the walls. We felt as though we'd discovered something new, that we were so trendy. And yet I didn't excel in exams. I felt as though I'd been born on the wrong side of the tracks. I had a chip on my shoulder and it held me back."

The divide that existed across Crewe communities became apparent to Rob as he grew up, and with his family's council house came a label. "Across the estate Sandiway Road and Windsor Avenue were known as the posh houses, mostly privately owned. We lived in a world of rent collectors, although they weren't too smart. They came at the same time each week and we were taught to avoid them. People had jobs but it always felt like a hand-to-mouth existence. We had gas and electric meters and we had to put a coin in the Radio Rentals TV. The houses were basic, the kitchen was bare brick and there was a Belfast sink. That was it, along with an outdoor toilet. Oh, and it was very cold in winter. It sounds like a Dickens novel, but it was so cold we'd use one of mum's coats as an extra cover. And there was little to stimulate kids' minds. In all my childhood I don't remember going into a single house and seeing a book. When you live in an environment like that you can see why many people don't leave, why they feel that they are not good enough. Someone needs to help break that cycle."

Rob (bottom right) with Wulvern F.C.

An opportunity to help make the necessary changes came years later in 2003 when social landlord Wulvern Housing took over the administration of the Crewe & Nantwich council stock. Having lived and worked away for several years Rob returned to Crewe, taking the role of Partnerships Director at the new organisation. "The complicated family arrangements I see today are nothing unusual; I lived the same life as a kid, and on the same estates. Wulvern is the kind of organisation that has a conscience and I believe there's a moral and ethical obligation to treat the people in our houses properly and fairly. You can give someone a set of keys, but they could step into a home where there will be poverty, reduced educational opportunities and crime. We need to create communities where people want to live and thrive. Transforming bricks and mortar is easy, but I think we can honestly say that we invest resources in the communities. That's one of the reasons I was attracted to the job. I've got the opportunity to help make a difference and I have no intention of wasting it..."

Queens Park cafe, Wulvern film, June 2008.

Christine Messam
The Jamaica Inn

In 1959 a chance meeting on Heathfield Avenue changed Christine Miller's life forever. Walking with friends she was introduced to a Jamaican man, and for her it was love at first sight. However, a 15-year age gap was always likely to raise eyebrows. The young Crewe girl faced a dilemma as family and friends rejected the idea of a relationship…

"There were six of us, all girls, and my dad was very strict. He was very protective and we weren't allowed to go too far from our Thomas Street home. If we did, and he found out, he'd beat us with a stick he kept in the cupboard! He was a tough, strong man who worked on the railways as a gatekeeper. It must have been strange for him spending most of his working day with men and coming home to a houseful of girls. So when I met Lester I suppose my dad saw him as a threat, someone who would take away one of his girls." However, with school complete Christine started working at CWS, a sewing factory on Camm Street. "It meant that I had a little money and some independence, and I started to see Lester when I could without getting caught. Eventually, I knew that I had to make a decision. So I moved to his house. There was shock and outrage. That's when most of my family cut me off."

Several tough years followed with Christine effectively ostracised by her mother and father and, sadly, most of the sisters that she had hoped would support her. Her family missed out on the birth of her first two children, but it

was the sound of wedding bells in 1963 that finally changed hearts and minds. "It was at my sister Eileen's wedding, and I was standing alone in the Christ Church doorway. Lester hadn't been invited so I'd gone over to my father to see if he'd talk with me. He hadn't noticed me arrive and I heard him ask my mother if I was coming. When he realised that I was standing by his side he just cried like a baby. He smiled and then hugged me. Lester and I were invited to tea that Sunday and my father realised what a decent man he was."

Christ Church was the setting for more confetti the following year, this time for the official union of Christine Miller and Lester Messam. "We married in 1964 when I was 21 years of age. Hundreds turned out on a beautiful July afternoon - friends and family plus a lot of fascinated bystanders. You didn't get many mixed marriages back then so I suppose it was something different. I was the centre of attention and, most important, all of my sisters were there to see me. Later, my father said that Lester was probably the best son-in-law a man could have – once he'd got used to him. He always said that you could see your face in Lester's shoes!"

Sadly, with the celebrations over, some decided to turn their backs on the newlyweds: "After the wedding a lot of people stopped talking to us, including some of my sisters. I think that other people influenced them, maybe neighbours and work colleagues. And yet there was very little prejudice from our neighbours or the people we worked with. It was my family more than the people of Crewe."

Christine's third and fourth children were born when the couple were running the Crown Hotel on Municipal Square. It was the start of another adventure, something completely new for them. "I'd hardly ever been in pubs let alone worked in one. It was something that Lester wanted to try, although he'd got no experience of the trade either. We just gave it a go and learnt as we went along. Most people we met accepted us, which was lovely. It became known as Jamaica Inn and we even had a visit from a man called Dick Pixley who was a radio reporter for a show called *Jamaican Rendez-Vous*. It used to make me smile thinking that people half way across the world would have listened to us talking about our pub back in Crewe."

Lester and Christine in the Crown, c1967.

Before long, however, the hectic environment of a pub wasn't right for a growing family. "We stayed just over three years at the Crown and enjoyed every minute of it, but we just needed to settle down. We moved to Samuel Street and made that part of Crewe our home. It was a friendly area in the 1970s, everyone said hello and there was a real sense of community. We felt safe and part of an extended family. Lester went to work at Rolls-Royce that was only a few hundred yards down the road and I remember seeing him cycle along West Street with hundreds of other men from the factory. I also worked and became a nurse at Leighton Hospital on nights to help pay the bills. In 1974 my family was complete when I gave birth to my fifth child, another baby daughter. Like my dad, Lester had a house full of girls – although we also had one boy!"

By the late 1980s, and with most aspects of family life settled, there was a huge decision for a woman who had hardly ever set foot outside Crewe. Lester went to Jamaica to visit old friends and came back with a proposal. He wanted to return to his homeland. "We didn't want to rush into anything, so we went on holiday there a few times. It was hot, slow moving and very different from England. I wasn't sure about it initially, but I knew that I wanted to be with my husband. So when Royce's offered redundancies in 1990 the time was right. We built a new home on some land that Lester owned with

The Messams on Samuel Street, 1972.

his sister on the south side of the island, a market town called Black River."

Sunnier climes help soften the blow, but having to leave children behind is the biggest wrench for any mother. "I hadn't seen too much of my sisters, only Eileen. So I didn't miss them. I was sad to leave Crewe, as it was all I had ever known, but it was being without my children that hurt the most. My youngest, Rachel, was only 16 years of age when we left. The others had moved on so we gave her a choice, but she decided to stay in Crewe with her brother and sisters. She had her own life to lead. I cried but it reminded me of myself all those years ago, making my own decisions. I'd love to come back to Crewe. I do miss it. But it wouldn't be with Lester because he won't come back again. He's settled and happy."

In the summer of 2009 there was a happy addendum to this story. Visiting Crewe for the first time in four years, to see her own children, a special get-together was also organised for Christine and her sisters. The Duke of Gloucester pub was the venue and gave Christine another glimpse of changing Crewe. However, it wasn't the place or the meal that mattered. "Seeing my sisters together again was like a dream. I hadn't seen two of them for many, many years, so sitting down and talking like a family was wonderful. We chatted about everything that night - memories, gossip and the little things that connect sisters. The tricks we played, places we visited, people we knew. Just chit-chat I suppose..."

Christine and her sisters, May 2009.

Shanaze Reade
Top of the World

The dusty track at Crewe's Tipkinder Park was the perfect place for kids to let off steam and throw bikes over mounds and around tight corners. One young girl loved it so much she quit hanging around the streets and dedicated her teenage life to BMX. A bumpy ride, but one that would see her race to the top of her game...

"From a young age I knew that I wanted to be involved in sport, but I never dreamt that it would involve bikes. At school I enjoyed athletics and I was a good sprinter. In the evenings and weekends there wasn't much to do around our streets, so I went along to Tipkinder with my cousins one day and paid a pound to hire a BMX bike. A bloke called Bob Field ran the club and his enthusiasm was infectious. He was known as Black Bob and had a massive Afro. Oh, and he was always smiling. Everyone was made welcome and he always had time to chat. Looking back, he was the reason I went back again and again."

Shanaze's parents split soon after she was born and much of her early life was spent with her grandparents, aunts and uncles. Hardly a wild child, but without focus who knows where this Crewe kid would have ended up? Instead, her dedication to BMX soon set her apart from others. "I started riding when I was ten and within

Tipkinder in the late 1990s.

a few months I was obsessed. I'd pack my bag the night before - my kit, drink and snacks - then head down to the track and grab any daylight time I could. It was great in the winter when hardly anyone else turned up, as I could practice everything over and over without interruption. As I grew and became more of an athlete I'd get down to Tipkinder at 6am in the summer to squeeze three hours in before school. It was the same in the afternoon, straight to the track getting in the training I knew I needed if I was going to succeed."

Bob Field at the starting gate.

The hard work paid off. At just 15 Shanaze became the World U18 BMX champion. Then, unexpectedly, there was some great news about her sport that encouraged her to put any idea of further education on the back burner. "When I started out BMX wasn't very high-profile and only a few people rode professionally. In 2003, when I was choosing GCSE subjects and trying to plan my future, my coach at the time, Jeremy Hayes, told me that BMX had been added to the 2008 Olympics in Beijing. It was nearly five years away but I knew immediately that I wanted to become Olympic Champion. So if there was a moment when I knew it would completely dominate my life, it was then."

From that moment it was a crazy regime of fitness work and practice - and often in unusual places. "The sprint training was important and that's how I improved my power. One of my favourite venues was Morrison's supermarket car park early in the morning. There was a good stretch where you could get a 100 metre run going. I used that to improve my times. People often gave me strange looks and a few asked me why I didn't go down to Tipkinder. I did that as well, but the flat surface was brilliant for speed work. One of the lads from the track, Levi Ashley, started training with me, then about 15 of us formed an unofficial club, all working together and improving our times."

A teenage girl, competing against and beating local lads, must have turned heads, but there was no animosity. "After a couple of years I was winning races. But everyone was cool about it. There was no jealousy as everyone at the club pulled together. Black Bob made sure of that. When you lose to someone, boy or girl, then that's your target - to beat them the next time. So although I hate losing it always gives me something to aim at the next time. The lads at Crewe just accepted me as one of them." Those closest to Shanaze have also been very supportive, helping her keep her feet firmly on the ground. "My family are very laid back. They treat me as they always have. Even when I've been top of my game and competing at massive competitions these are the people who keep me grounded. Winning tournaments makes them smile and they are proud, but I'm still just Shanaze to them. I don't get any special treatment from friends and family. That's how I like it. I want to remain a normal person."

For Shanaze there is no better place than the track, a place she can immerse herself in the single-minded pursuit of success. "There's nothing like a final, the last race of a long day. Your nerves are jangling and your heart is beating fast, but the last few seconds at the gates are amazing. You know the bar is going to drop but you're pushing forward, holding the front wheel tight against the gate. And that split second is vital. Get the edge at the start of a race and you're half way there. Anyone in the final is there on merit and about the same ability, with the same power. So any advantage at the start is what sets you apart and gives you the chance to dominate from the front. Then the race proper kicks in. All the preparation, the planning and practice is tested. You must avoid contact with the other riders as you hit the pedals, flat out as you dive to the bottom of the first slope. Then the jumps become priority and you have to be perfect. There are no second chances. Forty seconds of racing – up, over and around the berms. You have to be precise. Your mindset has to be spot on and you must know what you're doing over every part of the course. If something does go wrong you have to sort yourself out in seconds. But that's usually too late. So you work hard to avoid that situation. Getting over that finishing line - first - is everything."

In July 2007, in her first senior season, Shanaze became the Women's Senior UCI BMX World Champion. Lifting the ultimate crown, therefore, at the Beijing 2008 games seemed a formality, but a clash of bikes in a dramatic Olympic Final saw her walk away empty handed.

Shanaze with the Cheshire Ghost Riders.

That was a major disappointment, but coupled with the death of Black Bob a few months earlier she became more determined. "Losing in the final was a massive blow but it allowed me to take stock. Whenever I have doubts I think about Bob, because he was the one who always inspired me. He brought such a vibe to the track. It was fun and enjoyable. Without that I don't think I'd have spent so much time at Tipkinder or gone on to compete at the highest level. I was given something to focus upon, and I could set my own high targets. That hasn't changed.

People around me made me believe that I could achieve something. I don't think I'd had that before. So setbacks only serve to spur me on."

Olympic gold, perhaps at the 2012 London games, is still in her sights. However, a local tribute put a huge smile on Shanaze's face in August 2009 when the Tipkinder track was renamed. "It's a massive achievement and a great honour to have the track named after me. So many good riders have come through this track over the ten years that I have trained here, so to see my name on the sign feels fantastic. I think Bob would be proud."

Diane Dyer
Growing the Family Tree

One of Crewe's most prestigious factories was the backdrop for a romance that started Diane Dyer's family, but it was the passing of loved ones that encouraged her to delve deeper into her family's history. Her quest for information saw her become an integral part of a society that seeks to preserve the past for future generations...

"The first 20 years of my life were spent around the West End, living on Goulden Street, Barnabas Avenue and finally on Burlea Close. After school I wanted to be a nurse, following in mum's footsteps. She had trained at the old Memorial Hospital on Victoria Avenue. She called the newly built Leighton Hospital a 'biscuit factory' because people were processed, in one door and out the other. So she wanted me to study at North Staffs, but I discovered that I'd have to move over there to complete the training. That put me off, as I'm too much of a home bird to leave Crewe. So that was that."

With travel out of the question it was a case of picking through the limited choices open to young Crewe adults in the mid-1970s. "There weren't too many options when I left school. You either worked in a shop or an office. I applied to Rolls-Royce but they turned me down - because I was too quiet! I went to General Relays on Underwood Lane, working all day with a pair of pliers making telephone equipment. It was soul-destroying work but it paid £20 a week. Luckily, a month later I got a call from Royce's asking if I still wanted a job. I was shocked but delighted. It meant a pay cut, but the prospects were much better. So I started in the planning department, then spent a few months in other areas – as all starters had to. Oh, and making tea for hundreds of people formed a large part of the day! I eventually got a permanent place as a typist in the planning area and that's where I met my husband, Paul. I used to walk to work down Sunnybank, but he'd often pick me up in his mini."

Married in 1979, the family looked set to grow. But it was the loss of relatives close to Diane that eventually started an interest in the past. "The family research began after my great grandmother's funeral. She was buried at Crewe Cemetery and there was a huge get-together at the Imperial on Edleston Road. You see so many relatives at those occasions and they seem to know all about you. Aunties, uncles and cousins all say hello and tell you how much you have grown. You remember faces but the details are fuzzy. So I started trying to piece things together, assemble a family tree. It was just our immediate family at first, but I found some of it fascinating and I wanted to complete the bigger picture. I was working at the time and also expecting my first child, so the research was put on hold."

In fact, it would be four years before the project resumed. The death of a grandfather and, soon after, her closest grandmother was a traumatic period but drove Diane to find out more. "My mum went back to work when I was young, so I spent a lot of time with my grandmother. She taught me everything from cooking to knitting. Even when I left home and married I'd go and see her regularly. We were very close. It was a shock when she died and it felt as though a piece of me had been taken away. We had been trying for another child and she knew that we wanted a bigger family. So when the twins arrived nine months later we considered them to be a present from her. While they were at nursery school I met a couple of other mums who told me about a local group, the South Cheshire Family History Society. They met on a Friday night at the Christ Church Hall so we decided to make a night of it. To begin with it was a bit of fun, a social thing. People would meet half an hour before the formal presentations and also hang around after to chat and make new friends. They were all really helpful and they pointed you in the right direction to help your research. I hadn't expected it, but I was hooked from day one."

Diane's grandmother, Kathleen.

It was a casual arrangement at first, but within a few years Diane became formally involved. "They were always looking for volunteers. Initially, I helped out with some typing, updating details of monumental inscriptions. We'd get hand-written notes from other members and we entered the information onto computer. That was fine because I could do this while the kids were at school. My first proper project was up at St. Michael's in Coppenhall, and then later I did similar at Whitehouse Lane Cemetery in Nantwich. The headstone inscriptions are fascinating and offer so much more than simple dates and names you find on official registers. So capturing this kind of information is an important source of data that people can reference when looking to make the connections from the past. You always

Coppenhall Cemetery, October 2007.

have to go back to the original source, and that could be the headstone. It's so very sad that graves are often left to deteriorate and often disappear altogether. Unfortunately, when families move away, there is often nobody left to tend and maintain the graves. The council has a duty of care to look after the cemetery, but actual plots belong to the families. They are responsible. So what we do is important. You get ancestors from all over the world visiting and looking for information that they haven't been able to find on the Internet or in books. So the ongoing work to catalogue these personal details is vital."

The society has operated from three bases since its formation, but always in the heart of town. "In the 1990s I'd say that around 60-70 people attended the meetings at Christ Church. Because the numbers grew they moved to the Salvation Army Hall across the road, but this meant that the night we met had to change and a few people couldn't attend. So numbers dropped off a bit. Then in 2009 we were given another new home within Crewe library, which meant we were close to more research tools and also accessible to people. We like to call ourselves a learning resource; somewhere people can come and chat. So we're not quiet. That's why we're tucked away in our own room! The group is predominantly older people as they tend to have more time, but we do get younger members coming along - just as I did nearly fifteen years ago."

Although much has been achieved and documented, the work is far from complete. "Being involved with the society has introduced me to a lot of local history, so I suppose my love affair with Crewe has blossomed as I have uncovered more and more. There is no official archive in Crewe, and much of the information, photos and other records are held by private collectors. These people are passionate about the town but the wonderful collections are spread all over the place. If they could be brought together, in a central location, it could be a fantastic resource. So if I have a longer-term objective then it's to see somewhere created that people can visit, get hold of the details they need and perhaps learn about the people who have made Crewe what it is today. I hope I can help to achieve that."

South Cheshire Family History Society at Crewe Library, September 2009.

Toby Robinson
Jack of all Trades...

Some people never settle at school and avoid the steady careers that others plan for years in advance. After a series of random jobs, Toby Robinson grabbed an opportunity to enter local journalism and report on Crewe Alexandra, something that would offer him stability and open new doors...

"School didn't suit me, even as a young kid. Mum and dad worked so I used to go home at lunchtime from Hungerford Primary School. Other kids had school dinners or sandwiches, but I'd often go to the chippy at the top of Vincent Street. It was mad really, and looking back a young lad walking along busy roads was dangerous. But the best bit about those early days was the adventure playground. There was a scheme for children after school, at weekends and during the summer holidays. Kids came from all over the Sydney estate. They had Tarzan ropes, equipment to make things, ball games and activities run by play scheme workers. It taught us a lot - and it was fun. I don't think school children have the same freedom now, and the play area that was built years later is too sanitised, too safe to allow real creativity."

Despite being moved away from friends at Crewe schools during his teenage years, Toby was never destined to take an academic path. "I quit before I sat my GCSEs, so I left with nothing. Perhaps that was foolish, but I went through a rebellious phase. I have no regrets. I tried to sort myself out and enrolled at South Cheshire College, resitting exams I should have taken a year earlier. But I soon lapsed into the student lifestyle and spent a lot of my time drinking and playing pool in the Earl of Crewe pub on Nantwich Road. Eventually, I completed some NVQs but never wanted to take things further, like going to university. So I drifted into a series of temporary jobs, trying a bit of everything. People laughed because I went through about 15 jobs in a year. Then an administration role cropped up on the ninth floor of Rail House, working through an agency. It was just before British Rail was broken up and I remember seeing a letter recommending that I be offered a permanent position. So I nearly started a railway career, but the contract ended and things changed as parts of British Rail became Railtrack. So I ended up taking other temporary work elsewhere."

Then one of those too-good-to-be-true jobs was advertised. The local Crewe and Nantwich *Guardian* required a sports reporter, even offering training to the successful candidate. Despite a lack formal experience or qualifications Toby's local knowledge and love of Crewe Alexandra appealed to the newspaper. "The interview went really well. Everything about the role was perfect, although the money was less than I was earning on temporary railway jobs at the time, then I got a letter saying that I hadn't been successful. I was gutted. Luckily, within a year, I saw the position advertised again. I rang the editor immediately and he told me that he had been thinking about me. I'd been second choice first time around, but he asked if I was still interested. I didn't have to think about it. I went through another interview and at the second attempt I got the job."

The Guardian moved from its Market Street office in the late 1990s, so alongside the *Sentinel* and *Crewe Chronicle* the High Street area became Crewe's mini Fleet Street. "There was a good feeling about the place in the first few years. There were five of us on the paper's editorial side and I also had some great support from established journalists like Roy Greer (*Chronicle*) and Gwyn Griffiths (*Sentinel*). I think they appreciated that I cared about the Alex. It also helped that our editor, Mark Smith, liked the fact that I was passionate about the local sports scene, unlike others who had used the paper as a stepping stone. So I felt part of the team and started to cover the Alex during one of their most successful periods in the Championship. Without being big headed I think I managed to develop an informal style that people enjoyed reading. It wasn't quite a fanzine, nor was it the usual straight-laced

David Cameron and Edward Timpson in High Street.

format so common in most newspapers. I stuck at it, and with the editor's backing the sports section grew to several pages. Despite pressure from the sales teams we refused to buckle and maintained the format. I think the readers liked that."

The Alex staff also seemed at ease with the young journalist's style, although long-serving club manager Dario Gradi rarely let his defences down. "Dario told us what he wanted to tell us, although he wasn't the dominating ogre that some thought. That just wasn't the case. I never got close enough to know him that well, nor did we fall out. There was a mutual respect. John Fleet, the kit man, was a big help, always making us feel welcome, as did the other staff at Reaseheath. The players were different. They seemed to change during my time covering the club. They became less approachable. That was a shame as you often got the feeling that they wanted to speak out. It was hard to comprehend because I spent a lot of time with Steve Walters in my late teens. That was a fascinating period, seeing him develop as a player in the early 90s and as a man away from the game. Too many people thought that he was a hot head, a troublemaker. That wasn't really the case, as a lot of people picked fights with him because he was an up-and-coming star. So I saw a footballer's life up close and personal. Because of that, I tried to give other players a bit of space when I started reporting on the game."

Sadly, *The Guardian* couldn't avoid the major cutbacks and changes that swept through the newspaper industry as the Internet altered the way people accessed news. Ending a ten-year association with the paper might have broken many people, but Toby grabbed the opportunity when the axe fell in early 2009. "I had a philosophy that people read our paper predominantly for the Alex news, followed by the 'What's On' guide. I managed to increase the entertainment content and made some great contacts during my final year at the paper. I helped with promotional activities for the M Club, a club just down from the paper's High Street base. That involvement with the music industry encouraged me to establish an agency called Volume PR with my friend Mark. It was geared toward the local music scene and a natural progression was to set up a music festival for Crewe. It was something that had always frustrated me, seeing most large-scale events staged down the road in Nantwich. So we did something about it and the Crewe Live 08 music festival happened at the end of May, just after the by-election."

The event was a huge success and led to more work. "We teamed up with Ray Brushev from the Royal Hotel complex, which included a music venue at the back called The Box. He came to us and I'd like to say that we played a part in creating a Rock and Indie scene for Crewe, getting up-and-coming bands to the town alongside a number of decent local acts like Sgt Wolfbanger, Flux, Bleached Wail and the Sumo Kings. The 2009 Volume Festival raised the bar further and suddenly local pubs and other venues were copying our formula. I suppose that's flattering. I've no idea where I will be in five or ten years, but I'd hope to be in Crewe promoting music - maybe in a different form. We'll see…"

Toby at The Box ticket window.

Nick Bayes
Tower Struck Down

Nursing, managing a successful pub and driving delivery vans has helped to pay the bills, but playing the bass guitar has always been Nick Bayes' passion. From youth clubs to Crewe pubs, international tours to Glastonbury and more - it's been a proper rock 'n' roll ride. Years later, he's still knocking out tunes with old mates...

"My mum and dad grew up in Crewe, but dad's engineering work took him all over the world. In the late 60s they were living in the Lake District, but a few years after I was born we came back to Crewe and we settled on Gainsborough Road. My interest in music started soon after I went to Ruskin School, and yet it was my friends at Kings Grove who were starting to play in bands at the time. I played guitar but the bass fascinated me. That's what got me really hooked, so I started a band called Organised Chaos with a mate called Martin Thomasson. We were about 14 at the time and we couldn't get into the pubs, so our first gig was at the youth club on Browning Street. It was behind the Methodist Church and you went down some steps, almost into a basement. It was all teenagers like us, but it was a great first show, very boisterous as I remember. I played bass and worked a drum machine while Martin played guitar and sang. I always smile when I hear ZZ Top's Sharp Dressed Man, because that was our opening track. There's probably an embarrassing tape of it knocking around somewhere!"

Humble beginnings, but gigs would play a huge part in Nick's life. "Martin and I stayed together for several years and we had another band called Boomerang when we left school. It was a bigger set-up, with Heather Shepherd on keyboards and Ian Hayward on drums, and a singer called Simon Gibbs who went on to play in Angels With Dirty Faces. I think they had a number one in Japan in the early 90s! We played all over the town, including the Crewe Carnival in 1985. We also did a few gigs at the Naval Association on Eaton Street, but we spilt up, as young bands often do, and I was in limbo for a while."

Then came a bit of luck. Training to be a nurse and based at Leighton Hospital, it was the launch of a new music venue that grabbed Nick's imagination. "A guy called Mike Darlington had just bought the Leisure Club on Edleston Road. He was part of a really big musical family, and because

Nick at Whatfest, 2009.

they all had connections in the industry the club's music nights gained momentum quickly. I went along and jammed with some fantastic musicians, really talented people. So I started to learn and improve. The whole scene in Crewe stepped up a gear and bands were coming to the town from all over to play at the club. Other venues were putting live acts on, like Pinchers, the LMR and the Cheshire Cheese pub, but the Leisure Club really stood out. Around 1990 it was renamed and it became Micky D's. That's when I got involved with a band called Tower Struck Down. They were a well-established group with a punk/folk sound. They'd played all over the country during the 80s and Mark Callaghan, known as Cal, was the lead singer. He asked my mate, Neil, to audition for them but, for whatever reason, he said no. Still, he suggested that they gave me a shot at it. I was flattered and remember thinking they were out of my league. But I got the job!"

Involvement with a professional band meant giving up nursing, relentless practice and extensive touring - just what a young musician craved. "There'd been a hiatus before I joined and Cal was rebuilding the band. He was writing his own material and was heavily influenced by The Waterboys, a kind of Celtic sound. We spent some time rehearsing at the Darlington's farmhouse where Cal was living at the time. A bloke from Sandbach, Simon Mellor, became the drummer and Brendan Darlington eventually took over as the guitarist. We took the new line-up around the country for a while, but to complete the Celtic look and sound Cal wanted to recruit someone who could play a traditional folk instrument. Martin "Bunny" Wright was the answer as he brought the fiddle and banjo to the line-up, and that really took us down the folksy road. That's when we started to play the festivals and we did gigs the length and breadth of the country. We even travelled into Europe and had a regular following wherever we toured. They were great, wild times. We had the look of travellers and around that time a group of German hippies followed us from gig to gig, all over France. Martin quit while we were in France, and

Nick (left) with lead singer Cal.

while we were out there Brendan's brother joined the band. We had another fiddler from Macclesfield called Kate for a while but she left for family reasons. Thankfully, while touring in Northampton we met a girl called Clare Smith, who became known as Fluff, and she stayed throughout the rest of my time with the band. I suppose the high spots for me were supporting the late Kirsty MacColl and playing Glastonbury in 1993."

All good things come to an end and for Nick his family had to come first. "They were fantastic times, but when my son, Daniel, was born in 1993 it became very hard to fit everything in. I tried to carry on but the family was my priority, so I settled down and worked as a paramedic. I suppose I dipped out of the music scene for about five years, although I played the odd session here and there. I didn't get involved again until I divorced in 1999. The first thing I did was go out and buy a new bass guitar. It was one of those impulse decisions, a new start. I hooked up with Simon Mellor again, plus a guy called Ged Mitchell and we hit the pubs as a covers band. We eventually called ourselves Pantz! It was fun, made a few quid and fitted in around our jobs. I'd ended up running the Bear's Paw at Warmingham with my partner, Sarah, so a couple of gigs now and then were perfect. But I always hankered to be fully involved again, it just had to be the right project."

The pub stint came to an end in early 2008 and Nick and Sarah bought one of the newly converted flats in the former police training college off Nantwich Road. The day job involved driving a van, but an improving music scene kept his soul kicking. Then the Crewe Live 08 festival provided a great weekend of entertainment and also presented an opportunity. "Being able to wander from pub to pub, watching up-and-coming bands was superb. There was a great vibe around Nantwich Road, Mill Street and Edleston Road. I watched a band called Smart Girl & The Traxx and the lead singer was phenomenal. She had a stunning voice - and wrote her own songs. So I went to see her again at The Imperial the following day. Her name was Chloë Chadwick. A few months later she had split from her band and I bumped into her. We had a chat about the music industry and we just clicked. There was no intention to play bass with her, but that's what happened. We called the band Chloë and focused on her vocals. Who knows where it might lead? In the background I've teamed up with old mates Neil, Steve and Lee to play 70s and 80s covers under the name Foulplay, a bit of fun, just mates playing songs we love. And that's how I like it. It's what I've always done."

Foulplay.

Brian Silvester
A Life in Politics

It takes a certain persona to succeed in politics - at national or local level. Quite simply, Brian Silvester was made for the role. Nearly 40 years with the Conservative Party and continued commitment to local councils is testament to his staying power and desire to serve. There have been triumphs and disappointment, but no regrets...

Born in the house next to the landmark Churches Mansions building in Nantwich, the first tentative steps into education for Brian were at Manor Road School. "I wasn't at all keen on my first day. I was just five years old and took my opportunity to slip out and run all the way home. They made sure it didn't happen on my second day, and if similar occurred at a school these days there would be uproar." It makes for an amusing anecdote for a man who would later serve as a lay inspector of schools and also champion education during his year as Mayor of Crewe & Nantwich!

Nantwich and Acton Grammar School provided a good grounding for further education but it was not what the young man craved. "I joined the Young Conservatives when I was 17 years old and chose to leave education, initially working for my father in his Nantwich butcher's shop. I set up my own butcher's business in Crewe Market in the early 1970s but by then I had become very active in local politics. That's what really excited me. The new Crewe & Nantwich Borough Council was formed in 1974, and I stood for council in 1976, in the Shavington ward. Winning the seat was fantastic and I knew then that I'd be in politics for the long haul. I was only 24 so it was an exciting time. We took over from Labour and I was deputy chairman of a committee. It was a steep learning curve. In fact, there hadn't been a Conservative in Shavington before. It had always been an Independent ward. A few party members were worried about rocking the boat, but I won and never looked back."

The swing to the Conservatives provided the new councillor and his party with a number of meaty issues that provoked much debate. In fact, without some tough and momentous decision-making, an historic part of the town's landscape could have changed forever. "The railway cottages off Chester Street were earmarked for demolition by the Labour administration following years of slum clearance. People didn't want the cottages to go, so in 1976 we helped to save a vital piece of Crewe's heritage. That's something I have always been proud about."

Like many councils around the country, power switched between the political parties over subsequent decades. With Labour dominant in the 1990s and early part of the new century, the Crewe & Nantwich Conservatives had a battle on their hands convincing the voting public that change was required. The area had additional Labour influence in the form of local MP Gwyneth Dunwoody, who had been in power from 1974. Ultimately, a controversial civic decision was the catalyst for change.

Brian with Michael Howard, 1995.

"In 2006, as part of the proposals for a new shopping area, the Labour administration tried to push through the move of the Britannia war memorial from Market Square to the Municipal Square. The people of Crewe did not want that and they told us on the doorsteps as we campaigned. I think that the Labour party in Crewe & Nantwich had become complacent, whereas we had fresh ideas. We had to work hard but the time for change was right. We kept council tax charges down and still managed to sort out the mess surrounding the war memorial. Initially, I was against moving the memorial. But you must listen to the people. It is now in a fitting place and looks stunning, but the way it was moved was wrong."

In 2008 a decision was taken to alter the structure of local government, and with it came a controversial decision. Cheshire County Council would become two unitary authorities, with Crewe & Nantwich Borough Council and other authorities to be abolished. As such, it would be the last opportunity for one senior councillor to be mayor of the old borough. To much furore from opposition councillors a change to the convention was made that saw Brian installed as mayor. "I didn't see it as being controversial or wrong, it was an amendment to the convention and it was voted through democratically.

I was the longest serving councillor and I believe that it was the correct decision in light of the old borough coming to an end. Not everyone liked it, but that's politics. I have no regrets."

Whatever the circumstances nobody could suggest that the last mayor of C&NBC took his responsibilities lightly, recording 330 appearances at local events, supporting charities and organisations and promoting activities around the towns and villages. It was a humbling experience for the hardened politician. "You don't fully appreciate how much voluntary work goes on until you see it for yourself, every day of the week. There are some wonderful people out there. What stood out for me were the amazing acts of kindness that people do on a daily basis. There are thousands of unsung heroes, all trying to make a difference. The role of mayor is to support these people and recognise what they do. It was a privilege wearing the chain."

Mayoral duties aside, the arrival of Cheshire East Council brought a new role and fresh hope for Brian. "Only one government minister wanted to split Cheshire and yet it went through. Far from being a problem, it was a once in a lifetime opportunity for someone like me, helping to shape a new council from the start. I'm a politician through to my fingertips so this is what I'm in politics for, and there's a real opportunity for Crewe as part of Cheshire East. It's a huge authority, the third largest in the North West region and ninth largest in the country. Crewe is its biggest town and it has the industry, jobs and connections to become a major player in this part of the country. I want

Brian, William Hague and Sheila Davies - local elections 2007.

to be part of that challenge and hope to be associated with the new council for some time. The potential of Crewe is remarkable and if Cheshire East is to move forward then Crewe has to be involved and allowed to play a significant part."

For this to happen, and for Crewe to truly shine, a mayoral theme must be realised. "Crewe has needs, and there is recognised deprivation. It will need a lot of emphasis placed upon it and its services. During my time as mayor, the adopted theme for the year was Lifelong Learning. The standard of education is something that must be improved in Crewe. With the two-tier system gone there's an opportunity to take bold decisions and make things happen. The Ofsted league tables consistently show the Crewe schools behind those in, say, Nantwich and Sandbach. That's not good enough and I want to see that situation reversed."

So what does the councillor, one-time leader of the council and former mayor hope to be remembered for? "I never turn people away. I always try to help and I have a reputation for achieving things. So I hope that people appreciate what I have done and realise that it's been for the people of Crewe and Nantwich. I would be happy with that because I have always wanted to help improve the area."

Mayor Brian Silvester with Mayoress Sheila Davies, June 2008.

May Howard
Queen of the Washers

When a German torpedo hit HMS *Courageous* and claimed the life of May Howard's father in 1939, the teenager was forced to grow up quickly. Wartime Crewe toughened her and, despite much heartache, the era holds many fond memories. Fate and some bold decisions would ensure that Crewe would always be her home...

Born in 1924, May's childhood was spent in and around Queens Park. The family home was on nearby Davenham Crescent and the surrounding area was the perfect playground for inquisitive and mischievous kids. "We went to the park every day and knew every inch of it. It was a wonderful place, and we even found a way to make a few pennies. It was naughty really but we didn't think we were doing any harm. We found that one of the café's toilets had a penny slot in the door. Some people used this one even though they could use the others for nothing. So we put a few twigs in the slot and waited. People realised that the coins didn't drop and tried to get them out themselves, but it was very fiddly. We had small fingers and used a hair clip to get the pennies out. Then we spent them in the park's café. The lady on the counter used to look at our coins suspiciously. One day she asked why they had scratch marks all over them. So we stopped doing that before we got caught."

Perhaps it was the tough economic climate that dominated the 1930s, but even as a child May used her time and skills effectively. "While I was still a young girl, maybe 13, I loved to sing and dance. There was a local impresario called Lawrence Ratigan who organised the town hall dances. He also had a studio on Mill Street and I used money from running errands to pay for my lessons. I performed at Kettell's on High Street one night, impersonating film stars like Shirley Temple. But I had to get home before my father returned from his post office work around 10pm, so I left before they paid my cabaret fee. That would have been five shillings!"

As the Second World War gripped the nation, tragedy struck the Howard family. "My dad, a marine, was the first Crewe soldier killed in WW2, off the coast of Ireland in September 1939. Our house was filled with reporters wanting a story. It was a tough time, and my mum had to go out to work at Rolls-Royce to support us. I helped to look after my brother and sister, and people tried to make the war effort fun for the kids. One

May as a baby, with mother and father.

day, they asked everyone along Alton Street to help fill sand bags with buckets and spades." May avoided the early bombs that fell on Crewe, but an injury sustained during another air raid had dramatic results. "Mum was at work and I was looking after the children when the sirens sounded. I was still only fifteen and there must have been 20 raids around that time - one after another. So it was scary but you just dealt with it. We made our way to the shelter at the bottom of our garden in the dark. We always carried our little tins, with policies and valuables inside. I managed to get us down to the shelter but as I climbed in a burst of gunfire startled me. I lost my balance, slipped and damaged my back. I was taken to hospital in Chester where I stayed for two weeks. While I was there my mother took time off work to visit me. Her bosses didn't like that even though it was to see her poorly child, and they sacked her."

Tough times, and May continued to flirt with danger: "I was riding my bike with friends up near the Tipkinder mound one day and a dogfight was going on above us. The guns stationed at Tipkinder were firing at the enemy planes. Pieces of shrapnel were dropping to the ground, just missing our tyres as we rode. We could have been killed that day." Later the same year, a German bomber was successful. "It was a Sunday afternoon and we were out walking. We saw an enemy plane fly over, closer than usual, and we saw it drop its bombs. The Rolls-Royce factory was hit and sixteen people were killed. One of the unfortunate workers was the girl who had taken my mother's job after she had been sacked."

Subsequent years were dominated by queues, shortages and places to shelter when sirens shattered the silence. "We sometimes went to the Odeon if we had any money. If there was a raid you could stay there or go to one of the other shelters. There was one beneath Boots in the centre of town. There were bails of straw down there and we often mucked about, fighting with each other. Some of the older people didn't like us fooling around, so we had to move on some nights. We'd go to the Delamere Street shelter and you could see people's faces drop when a bunch of unruly teenagers walked in!"

Despite the ongoing turmoil there was more instability for May, as her mother moved the family to Edinburgh. The war effort, however, was never far away. "Within a year of moving to Scotland my call-up papers arrived with a posting to a powder factory in Glamorgan, Wales. Another girl said that the powder would turn my face yellow, so I didn't want to go there. Instead, I jumped on a train and headed back to Crewe to visit my auntie. Luckily, I managed to get at job at Royce's. The Ministry of Defence police wrote to my aunt checking up, but they never came to get me. So at the factory I worked on a lathe and they taught me on the job. I made washers and I called myself the 'Queen of the Washers'. There were a lot of women at the factory, but most of the managers were men. You often heard them asking girls out on a date and promising them better jobs. When you saw someone promoted or moved to an easy job the gossip was always about what the girl must have done to get it! I wasn't there long, probably about two years in all and then we got our release papers. The girls had come from all over the country and I met some great friends."

With her wartime work complete, May's transient existence continued. She returned to her mother in Edinburgh before the family moved down to London. The capital's bright lights, however, were not for May. "I applied to join the Wrens hoping to escape London, then travelled back to Crewe while I waited for my papers. I stayed with my friend Zona

May in 1938.

who lived above her father's shop on High Street. One night we went to a town hall dance and I met a wonderful gentleman. We talked and danced all night. He had two children and had lost his wife to TB. So I was cautious, but he was the one for me. I wasn't accepted by the Wrens, so perhaps staying in Crewe and getting married was meant to be."

A lifetime living and working around the Crewe area followed, but May still managed to keep in touch with some of the girls she had worked with during the war. Then, in 2005, flicking through a catalogue she noticed a blanket sporting a picture of a Spitfire and an idea was born. "I started the Spitfire Club, an informal group for the girls, as soon as I saw that blanket. A few of my old friends had died, but I sent these blankets to the rest of them - all over the world. It keeps the memories alive, so I have also given them to children of friends and family who otherwise wouldn't know anything about the Spitfire engines we made at Crewe. I have always thought that we should be proud about that."

The Streamline Revue, 1936. May is the one with writing on her leg!

Andy Gilbert
Thin Blue Lines

With two generations of his family earning a crust at Crewe Works, it was no surprise that Andy Gilbert choose a similar path and spent his working life around the railway. His career, however, took him along official lines as he policed the tracks, station and other buildings dotted around the sprawling railway land of the town…

"I spent most of my early life growing up around Lord Street. It was old railway housing, something that's been close to the family for as long as I can remember. Dad was from Crewe and earned his living in Crewe Works. Mum was from Newcastle-under-Lyme, so he moved out there for a while when they got together. He caught the train that used to go from Longport straight into Crewe Works. When they decided to stop that service he had to move back to Crewe. I was about two years old then. I went to the Edleston Road School that has now closed and is used by South Cheshire College, then on to Ruskin School when I was older. So everything I did was around the St. John's ward of the town."

The family's railway connections are considerable, something that would ultimately influence Andy's career choice. "My granddad was in the foundry, roughly where Hops bar is today, over the road from Christ Church and down from the Chester Bridge offices. That was back in the 1930s. My dad also went into Crewe Works in 1967 and served his time, before working at Ponds Garage on Nantwich Road. I didn't have a clue about my future, until one night when I was sat having a pint in the British Lion with my dad and one of his mates, Arthur, a serving Transport Police inspector. He suggested the railway police, so I asked him to get me the application forms. And that was that. I was sent to Cwmbran in Wales for 15 weeks of training. After that rookies were sent around the country to take up their first posts. Amazingly, I was allocated the Crewe office. So I only spent a few months away from the town."

In at the deep end, it was silly season and increased numbers on Crewe Station provided the early challenges. "My first active role was on the station over Christmas 1992. It was party season, drunks, fancy dress and travellers falling asleep on trains and on the platforms! It's fantastic really, as we don't spend our time on the streets like regular officers. We don't see the worst of it. The bars on the station tend to be closed by kicking out time so it's a case of getting people away from the station itself, watching over the taxi ranks. When you're stone-cold sober it can be amusing watching people trying to read timetables and count change!"

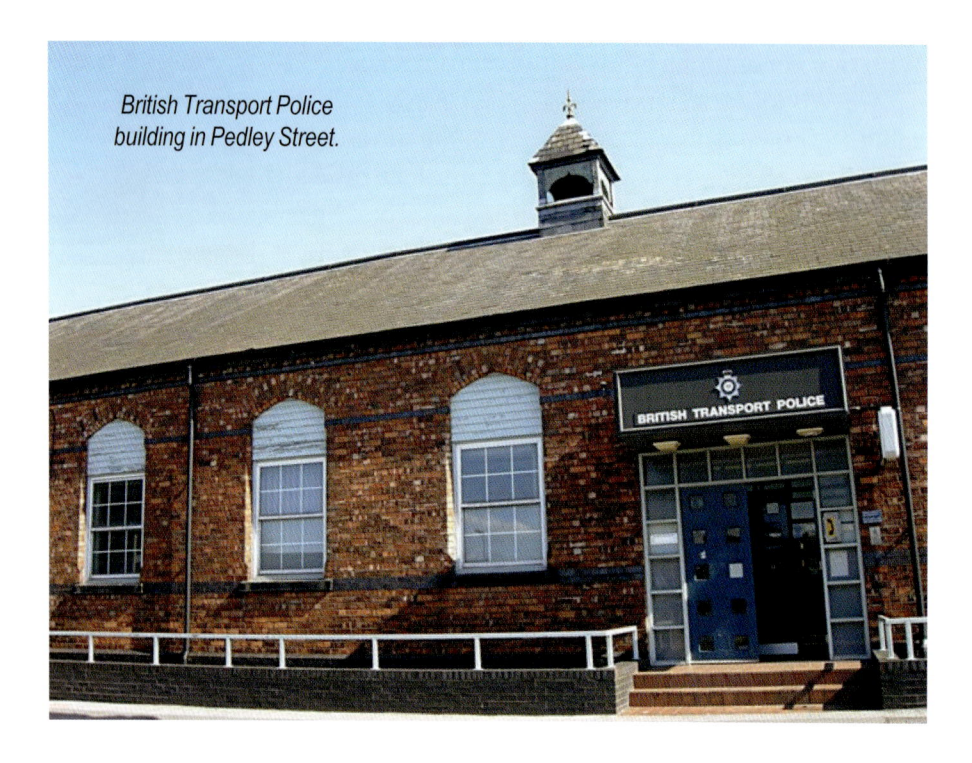

British Transport Police building in Pedley Street.

The station provided the unit's base for a number of years, but a move to one of Crewe's historic buildings brought back childhood memories for the young officer. "When I joined up the office was where the new Virgin First Class Lounge is now, on the main station concourse. A few years later we moved to the old Pedley Street School, where my dad went as a kid. While he worked for the railways he took me there to show me what it was like. They used it as a paper store in the early 80s, piles and piles of dusty old paper. As a kid it looked like mountains of the stuff. So when they told us that our BTP office was moving there it was a bit of a shock. All I remembered was how dirty it was, the rats, pigeons and musty smell. But it was soon cleaned up."

Joining the force helped Andy grow up quickly, but with it came a few interesting confrontations. "The job gave me a lot of credibility and respect from family and friends. And yet I did lose friends I'd knocked around with as a teenager, simply because I became a railway official. I realised that I had to change some of my habits and avoid old haunts. Spending 15 weeks away on training seemed to change things and people looked at me in a different way, maybe like some look at their mates when they return from university. A barrier has been put up and some tried to exclude me. Before I joined up we all went in the Express and the Barrel - Friday, Saturday and Sunday nights! That had to change. I also had to watch my back sometimes, especially around the old Pinchers Nightclub near our office. There were a few scary moments around the back of there. It's also strange being on the other side of the fence, as I've played in bands since I was young. So I'm often in places like Square One and The Box club, on stage, looking out on the audience, sometimes with people I've had to speak to when I'm on duty. I've been lucky, I suppose, because I know Bobbies who have been badly assaulted by lads we all knew at school. That's sad, but like most aspects of the job it's something that you have to handle as and when it happens."

Whilst old friends have changed, the area covered on the BTP beat has also been transformed over the years, with much of the old Works disappearing. "I've covered most of the tracks and buildings since I became a railway policeman, like the old coal yard down on Thomas Street, and the old cooling pools off Wistason Road, where the forge materials were cooled. That's also near where the British Rail training school once stood. My dad learned his trade there. Now there is a massive fishing pool, created by the lads who work there. You have to go over the tracks that feed the old sheds, but beyond them and near to the Chester Line you discover this fantastic pool. It's an incredibly tranquil place, a little oasis in the middle of the industrial area. It's beautiful."

One side of railway police business is neither exciting nor pleasant - dealing with trackside injuries. "Fatalities around Crewe are few and far between. For years most kids knew someone who worked on the railway, be it father, uncle or family friend. So people knew how dangerous things were and that trespassing on the lines would bring shame to the family. That's changed as less people work directly for the railways these days. Also, there are a few short cuts around Crewe that encourage people to walk along the tracks. About ten years ago a lad fell down an embankment behind the Grand Junction Retail Park. He told us that he had been out drinking and was walking home when he was chased by a gang of lads. He fell and came into contact with the overhead cables. The fall caused some broken bones as he landed on the tracks. Then a train hit him! It was a miracle he survived."

Whatever daily incidents arise Andy is happy with his chosen career path. "I can honestly say that I love the job, and yet things have changed more than you can imagine. These days we go out looking like soldiers, wearing combat trousers, batons and stab proof vests. When I started it was more reserved, like you'd imagine Dixon of Dock Green, cuffs and truncheons hidden away, notebook in top pocket and awkward helmet. Times have certainly changed, but all being well I'll being doing this until I retire..."

With his band SWaY at Square One, May 2009.

Nadia Dawson
On the Buses

For many years Crewe's railway hub and Works was famous across the nation, but Crosville Buses dominated the local transport scene. Nadia Dawson joined the company that spanned Cheshire and North Wales and, despite deregulation and threats of closure, has continued to help travellers make connections for almost 30 years…

"The bus station was opened in 1960, the year I was born. As a kid I'd come here to see where my dad worked, and it seemed huge to me. Everything looked clean and modern. I started to train as an optician when I left school, in one of the units just down the steps by Royal Arcade, but my dad tipped me off about a job here. I was saving up to get married at the time, on a pittance of a wage. Crosville operated the place back then, as they had when buses ran from Market Square. They were considered to be a good company to work for, so coming here seemed a sensible option to me. I started in May 1980 and worked alongside two fantastic people – John Keegan, who had been a bus driver for years, and the loveliest lady called Betty Shaw who eventually served 45 years on the buses in some capacity. She started on Queen Street when Crosville had an office by their old depot. This place really was her life."

Although most passengers spend just a few minutes waiting at the bus station, the people who work there have a habit of returning and spending many years at the interchange. "It's no surprise that bus drivers, maintenance crews and office staff stay and often form relationships. During my time I have noticed that people will leave to try something new but they always return in the end. There is something that lures you back in. If you have been away, you'll always come back and see some friendly faces. They are good people, and it's always been a great place to work. It's not got the same prestige that it once had, on a par with Royce's and Crewe Works as it was in the 1970s and 80s, and yet there is still a lot of pride here. My father always said that if you leave a company make sure that you depart in the manner in which you'd like to return. So we see many drivers coming back here, because they are decent folk. The place is a hub, not only for buses and customers, but also for the many people who work here. It's great seeing them drop by, even on their days off."

A strong bond exists between staff at the site, with an increasingly multi-cultural mix making working lives much more interesting and productive. "The demographic has changed a lot in recent years. There are around two hundred drivers who use the station, working for various operators. There are several languages spoken and you often hear conversations that combine two or more! The Polish drivers have been a tremendous help, especially with the growing community around the town. When the Polish and eastern European travellers have needed help they have always been happy to step in and assist me, making sure that they get the best possible service. I think it shows that we're an effective team, and that we care. Most of them have come here with good English and they are trying to improve themselves all of the time. In fact, when the roads were covered in ice and snow I remember a number of older passengers delighted to see a Polish driver at the wheel. They knew he was going to cope with the weather and conditions as they had more experience of extreme weather conditions around Eastern Europe. So it's been great to see such a mix of people working here."

Even being held captive doesn't seem to deter the drivers, as one amusing incident of inconvenience highlights. "There have been some bizarre days on the bus station. Once, two old ladies came over to the office with a piece of waxy toilet paper. They told us that they could hear banging from within the toilet block. Some building work was taking place that day around the shops off Tower Way and there had been the constant noise of hammers and drills. So we hadn't noticed anything unusual. When I looked at the paper it had some writing on it. A bus driver was locked inside and had passed the note under the door, asking passers by to come and speak to me in the office. Sure enough, when we walked over, there was a thudding coming from the toilet. He'd been trapped in there for over an hour! He survived, ego a little bruised, but he's still a driver here."

The incredible variety of customers will never cease to amaze Nadia, all of them with different stories to tell and varying reasons for using the buses. "There's a network of people who use our services regularly and I'd say that they are more considerate than others. People who give up their car for a day tend to be more demanding, more irksome. They don't appreciate the problems drivers encounter, often out of their control. Then we have regulars who love to keep me updated about their lives and will often wait for the next bus so they can stop for a chat. I've even met old ladies who were in the French Resistance! You just need to ask in order to learn about people. That stimulates me. Then there are the official guests, like the visit of Conservative leader David Cameron during the 2008 by-election. We were a little upset that the place didn't look its best, but I did manage to get a handshake. He was positive about what his party would do for the transport system, and it's nice when they make the effort to come and see us. There was tight security that day, but it was nothing to the drama of a few years ago when we had a bomb scare. We had to evacuate the station and head to the Delamere Street car park. When it happened I thought it would be chaos, but it was surprisingly easy - mainly because of the older passengers who reacted very calmly and guided the youngsters to safety."

The location of the bus station has been debated for years and numerous schemes have promised redevelopment. Successive councils have failed to start the regeneration, and a private scheme incorporating the town centre has also stalled. "They have talked about changes since the day I started here. I think there's a case for having the bus station in the centre, maybe just outside the main shopping core. But I hope they keep something close enough so that the people who really need the services are not prevented from getting around Crewe. For years we have only asked for the place to be brightened up and, to be fair, there has been some progress. One of the best schemes was a community project funded by Crewe companies and organisations. Kids and local artists created pieces of art that covered many of the walls around the station. They also took pictures of local people and drivers and made a mosaic of them for people to look at as they waited for buses. I think being able to identify faces from the town was a great idea and I'd like to see that repeated. It's easy to moan about how a place looks but to me it has always been about the people who come here. They are more important than bricks, concrete and a few fancy signs. Look after them and the rest will follow."

Mike Ramm
Making 'em Laugh

Always out for a laugh, Mike Ramm grew up on a diet of TV comedy thanks to a cool mum. With a proper job under his belt, the opportunity to promote local comedy gigs as a 'hobby' with his best mate was too much to resist. Within a few years international acts were playing to big audiences in Crewe...

"We came to the town when my mum started a course at Crewe & Alsager Teacher Training College, that was before it became MMU Cheshire. We lived on Samuel Street during my teenage years, and I got my first job at Westside Video while I was studying at Dane Bank College. It was a brilliant place to work. There were thousands of films to watch and people wanting to chat about movies, comedy and music. A fantastic fella called Pete Davis owned the store. His lad, Steve, was playing in the Premiership for Barnsley at the time. He'd pop in when he wasn't training and was just as friendly as his old man. It's great to see him back in the town as the Crewe Alex assistant manager."

College and part-time work was followed by a brief job in Stoke, before a steady career developed back in Crewe at 20:20 Logistics on the Weston Road industrial estate. Entertainment, however, was an ongoing passion. "Comedy was a major part of growing up for me. I watched Lenny Henry, Jasper Carrot and Alexei Sayle on TV. My mum was pretty cool and used to take me to the Midnight Comedy at Chester, seeing comedians like Alan Davis and Jeremy Hardy. So by the age of fifteen I'd seen cutting edge acts and was fully politicised! This carried on into my twenties as a group of us travelled around the region watching shows. Then a couple of friends, Wayne Williams and Scott Hanratty, started the Limelight Comedy in 2003. The club on Hightown was booming with tribute bands at the time and the café bar was the perfect venue to stage comedy. Wayne had visited 'The Comedy Store' in London and thought it would work in Crewe. So they were bold enough to give it a go."

Bringing a monthly show to the Limelight proved popular, with regular sell-outs encouraging some well-known acts to the club. "Things were going great and a bunch of us attended every gig. It was fantastic having quality comedy on the doorstep, but then Scott dropped off and left Wayne to run the show alone. That would have been fine, but Wayne didn't want to stand still and branched out with a bi-monthly open microphone night. It didn't really work and the overall audience declined. With hindsight, having two nights each month was too often for a town the size of Crewe. It wasn't big enough to support that, nor was the quality of acts good enough to bring people in from outside the area. As numbers fell the budget dropped. That probably forced Wayne to have a rethink."

In the event, an opportunity arose to take over the Limelight Comedy - a ready-made gig with bags of potential. "There are shows closing all the time – right across the country. I didn't want that to happen in Crewe. I'd been watching comedy for years with my mate, Jon Mitchell, and we had similar tastes. We reckoned we knew what would work, so when Wayne moved to Cheltenham with his partner there was an opening. Jon and I talked to our girlfriends and they were supportive. A promoter from Stoke-on-Trent had his eye on it, but we stepped in. He was livid that Wayne let two blokes from the audience take it over. As it happened, his shows have all finished!"

So the Limelight Comedy survived and the new duo relaunched with a high-profile star. "We took over towards the end of 2005 and Wayne had already booked Justin Moorhouse from Phoenix Nights, so we had a fantastic start. The crowd loved it and we worked hard to keep that momentum going. The highlights for us were getting up-and-coming acts and keeping tickets prices much lower than city venues. We had some stunning acts like Mark Watson, who went on to do the Magners TV adverts, then Rhod Gilbert who was massive all over the country with his Award-winning Mince Pie tour. Then Jim Jeffries played to around 100 delighted fans at the Limey, before travelling to Belfast and an audience of 1800. So that was a real winner for us. We got most of the acts because of the relationship we'd developed with agents and other comedians. We had a solid reputation and people trusted us."

In fact, maintaining a consistent standard became a trademark. "The Manchester and Liverpool clubs get large groups, stag and hen parties that want to cheer and shout. The Crewe gigs tended to be the same people who genuinely enjoyed comedy. It worked well for us and comedians talk to each other on tour, so it wasn't long before they started to approach us. They knew that the gig would run smoothly, although they might not get paid as much. But they could deliver their material without idiots ruining it. That wins every time. In fact, although other audience members might be amused, hecklers are a nightmare. We've been lucky and only had a few. If you get a witty heckler you're onto a winner, the comedian loves it and the whole atmosphere is improved. Unfortunately, the vast majority are drunks who would never normally speak out in front of hundreds of people. Their defences are down and the act on stage usually makes them look completely stupid. But like other distractions it can also ruin a show."

The Limelight Comedy reached its peak in mid-2008 with regular sell-out gigs encouraging Mike and Jon to expand. "We wanted to increase the audience to get even bigger names to Crewe. The final show at the Limelight, the 5th birthday gig, justified the decision to look elsewhere. We decided to use the band room downstairs and sold 300 tickets. It was packed but it wasn't right for comedy. People talked, walked past tables to the bar and caused too many distractions. That can destroy a night. So we moved to the M Club on High Street, the former Apollo cinema. That was perfect, plenty of space for tables all on one level and a custom-built stage that elevated the acts. A number of venues had approached us when we announced that we were leaving the Limelight. Being able to attract a consistent audience of 150-plus people is a big draw. It guarantees money over the bar. We rebranded the night 'M comedy' and planned for crowds of 275. That gave us scope to target some real mega stars on the circuit."

The first M Comedy gig was a sell-out, with internationally acclaimed Reginald Hunter headlining a top show featuring four superb acts. The switch to High Street also saw a move to Friday nights and capacity crowds were the norm. So where next for the Crewe comedy scene? "A lot of our audience comes from outside the area, so although there is a local scene I think there's scope for much more. Even during a recession people want to go out, to be distracted from the doom and gloom. Just going out to the pub can lose its appeal and customers want more. It's been a hobby for us but we love doing it, especially when we enjoy fantastically successful nights. There are worse things to be involved with than bunch of funny guys making people laugh. Hopefully we'll carry on for years. It's just a case of where…"

Mike and Jon Mitchell.

Gary Delaney
The Railroaders

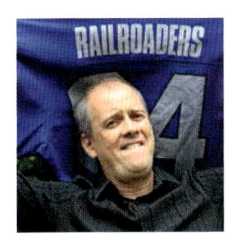

The end of the 1970s saw one young man return to Crewe in need of stability and a fresh start. A trusting stepfather made a job at Rolls-Royce possible for teenager Gary Delaney - and he grabbed the opportunity. Marriage followed, but a crazy dream soon dominated his life…

"My parents divorced when I was very young and my mother brought me to Crewe to start over with my 'new' father. I was a difficult child and tested my parents to the limit. Eventually, I moved to Suffolk to live with my real father. Things went from bad to worse as I neglected my education, missed lessons, flunked exams and left school with almost no qualifications. I needed to sort my life out."

With few options remaining, Gary returned to his mum in Crewe. "I was lucky, and thanks to my stepfather's clout I enjoyed a fast-track route onto the craft apprenticeship scheme at Royce's in 1977. I completed all of the disciplines, from milling and mechanics to electrical work and coach building. Then, in 1980, I won the Lord Hives Award - the highest honour bestowed on the company's craft apprentices. That helped me repay a debt to my stepfather. Deep down, I think he was proud of my award."

Some exciting times followed in the experimental department, developing a new car that would use a smaller BMW engine. Work dominated but there was room for another obsession. "The career opening up was great, but from the early 80s something else took hold of me - American Football. Channel 4 started to broadcast games in 1982 and I also tuned my radio to the American Armed Forces network for the live games. The reception was rubbish so I'd sit there waving the aerial around trying to get a signal. You'd have a Spanish Opera singer fading in over the commentary, but I loved grabbing any snippets I could."

By now married and living on Queens Park Gardens, a chance purchase by his wife fuelled his new passion. "She bought me a new magazine called *Gridiron UK*, instead of my preferred *Touchdown*. It was all about the British American Football scene. I had no idea there were teams starting up over here, so I was excited and wanted to be part of this new revolutionary movement. I still hadn't passed my driving test so getting to train with teams in

Stafford or Manchester was out of the question. So I decided to start my own team in Crewe, which was a crazy idea. So that's what I did; I became the self-imposed owner and Head Coach of the Crewe Railroaders American Football Team."

Setting up a new team in a railway town dominated by traditional sports was always going to be tough, but there were also some serious financial pressures. "We were struggling at the time with bills and mortgage payments. I'd tried loads of daft get-rich-quick schemes and my wife's patience was wearing thin. The last thing she needed was our spare cash devoted to American Football. Lads from the local rugby and football teams thought that we were idiots, and the fact that I was weedy and about eight stone soaking wet made it all the more laughable."

Still, a few friends and work colleagues were drafted in and an embryonic club was established. "There was no real backing from anyone official; in fact most of the people I spoke with thought I was bonkers - including my parents. I put posters up around town and gave the local papers a bit of flannel. I said we'd have proper American players coming to join the team in Crewe. I had big plans, but convincing anyone that this new American Football lark was going to be huge wasn't easy. Eventually, on a cold, wet November afternoon in 1984, we had our first Crewe Railroaders training session. Eleven guys turned up and, amazingly, ten of them would go on to

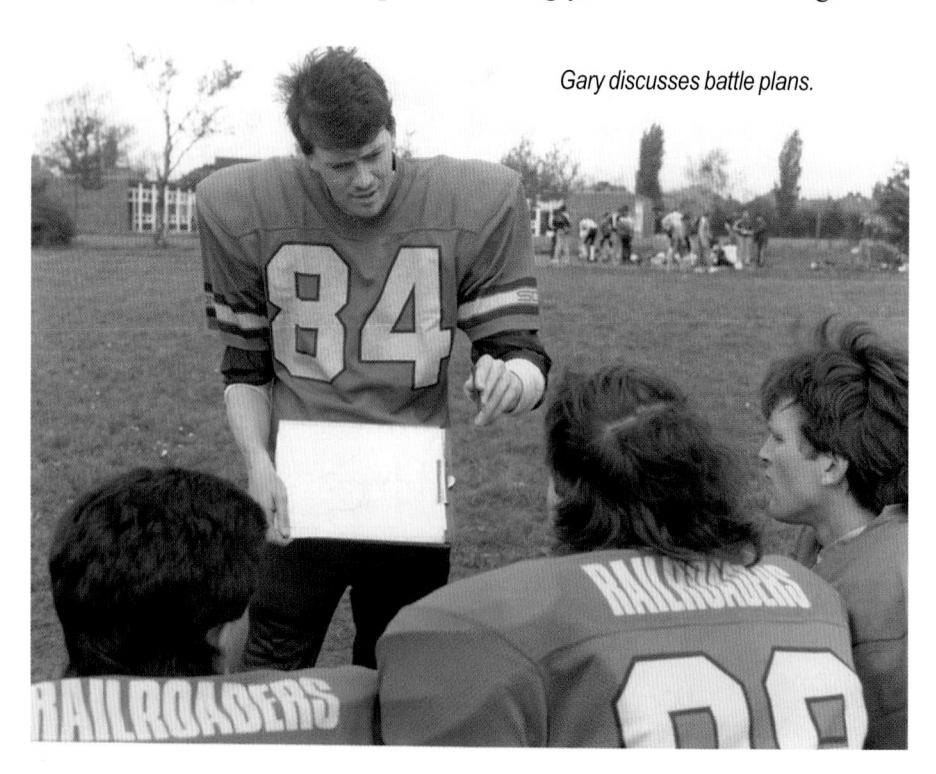

Gary discusses battle plans.

play in the first game in June the following year."

Securing a regular venue wasn't easy and it took parliamentary intervention to get things moving for the Railroaders. "The local council was apposed to us using the new Cumberland Arena. It was the flagship sports facility, but nobody was using it. I was furious when they wouldn't let us hire it. They probably thought we were a bit of a freak show. So I wrote to local MP Gwyneth Dunwoody. She appreciated that we were going to represent Crewe all over the country and, hey presto, within a couple of weeks we were offered the Cumberland as our home venue - and at a decent discount as well."

With the dream still alive a family was born, a group of players who would look out for each other. "If any of us were in trouble the whole team would respond and help. We had all invested hundreds of pounds of our own money to take part in the first recorded season of American Football played on these shores. It was quite comical at times, and I remember the first game when we didn't realise that everyone had to wear gum shields. The referees wouldn't let us play without one, so we had to share! One player would run off the field, take the gum shield out of his mouth dripping in saliva, and another would snatch it and pop it into his own mouth."

Everything about the team was close-knit, and social occasions were never dull. "It was very interesting going out in the evening for a drink en masse. We all wore black and silver jackets with 'CREWE RAILROADERS AMERICAN FOOTBALL CLUB' embroidered on the back in large letters. That always attracted attention, not always from young ladies! On many occasions we were subjected to abuse by a few drunks who fancied their chances, but they found out the hard way that if you took on one player you took on the whole Railroader family. Nothing usually happened, because once twenty or thirty big guys surround you most tend to realise that the odds are not in their favour."

On and off the pitch the Railroaders were a decent bunch and they made visiting teams welcome. "After the games we always had a few drinks with the opposing players. The Crewe Squash Club by the King George V playing fields and the Belle Vue on Earle Street were our favourite meeting places. Despite being a very violent and dangerous game, once the final whistle blew there was never any hard feelings or grudges carried over. We were all part of something new despite being on different sides. Other teams loved travelling to Crewe as we always put on a good spread after each game. When we didn't have a game on we used to dine at Rockafellas on Hightown, which had an American theme to it. I used to love their Wild West Smokey Burger dripping in barbecue sauce."

For Gary, however, the story didn't end in the 80s. He continued playing until 1993 and made some great friends along the way "The best thing about the Railroaders is that most of us have kept in touch; we still are a family. We still meet up for drinks, BBQs and the odd party. Years later, still a keen fan of the sport and encouraged by friends I decided to write about the Crewe experience. The book turned into a script, and after several years it's going to be made into a film called Gridiron UK, based on the true story of the formation of the Crewe Railroaders. We'll relive those wonderful years again and have our moment of fame, this time on the silver screen. Hopefully, it will put Crewe on the Hollywood map."

Gridiron UK filming is scheduled for April 2010, featuring actual locations used in 1985. It will be released at cinemas in November 2010, with a premiere in Crewe.

Gary with executive producer Gareth Jones.

Kevin Street
Teaching the Game

In the early 1990s a young kid trained long and hard in the shadow of Crewe Alexandra's old wooden stand. Kevin Street was destined to be a professional footballer and scored his first league goal on his Alex debut. The Westender enjoyed a few decent seasons but had to make some life-changing decisions in his footballing prime...

"I started kicking a ball around with my dad and some neighbours when I was about five years old. The other lads were always older than me, and I liked that. It was good competition and I think it helped me develop my strength and skill. We lived on West Street and played on the gardens with trees that were perfect for goal posts. Then we'd go over to the King George V playing fields, doing sprint training, kicking a ball against the walls of the pavilion changing rooms and then having a game with any kids who were there. I still go back there to do fitness work, remembering the great times we had. You don't seem to see as many children playing these days, but there were loads of us always wanting to play."

The informal games soon became serious, as school and county teams snapped up the talented player. Then the Alex coaches spotted his ability and the hard graft started in earnest. "The training facilities at the Alex were great compared to other pitches around the town. But when you compare the old Astro to the modern 3G pitches kids play on today then you could say we had it tough. It was as hard as concrete, with a coarse sandy top surface. If you went over you knew about it. Dario Gradi was there, pushing you to the limit, encouraging, criticising and making sure that you were reaching your potential. John Fleet was always helping out, taking training and keeping on top of the kits and equipment. We didn't have a changing room when we played next to the main stand, so we changed in the first team's dressing room. That was a big treat and it made the local lads smile."

The renowned Crewe Alexandra academy almost missed out on another starlet when back problems threatened to curtail Kevin's short career. "At 15 a painful injury forced me to take a year off. I was in agony for months and I wonder if those hard surfaces and unforgiving early Astro pitches contributed? Oh, and playing far too much football as a young lad! So I rested and, thanks to mum and dad, kept the faith and always believed that I'd get through it and eventually succeed as a player. I had doubts, for sure, and even considered putting my career on hold to concentrate on study. I figured that I could go to university and then carry on playing non-league football. But the Alex also had belief in me. I was offered a place on the Youth Training Scheme and never looked back."

That renewed confidence took him to the brink of first-team football in 1997, but he was forced to watch from the sidelines as a successful Alex squad secured promotion to the second tier of English football courtesy of a dramatic play-off final victory at the old Wembley stadium. His big chance finally came pre-season that summer. "I was desperate to play and knew I had a chance after some good performances during the pre-season. Then, in September of our first season at that level, I came on as a substitute versus Tranmere and scored on my full debut. I can't describe that feeling, to score the winning goal that secured three points for the team. I was always a fan so it meant just as much to me as the supporters on the sidelines. I think my dad was very proud as well."

The next few seasons brought mixed results for both Kevin and the Alex. Relegation in May 2002 was a harsh blow for the club, but it also marked the end of his career at Crewe. "Things were not working out for me. I'd had chances, done okay but never excelled. I don't think that I was improving as a player. Dario was always very forthright and he told me as much when we sat down and chatted at the end of the season. It was time to go. To be fair to the boss, he was fantastic and told me I could train with the club and even start some coaching. So that's what I did. The idea of university also resurfaced and I started to map things out."

The immediate future involved more professional football, but perhaps the biggest changes happened when Kevin dropped to the non-league scene with Stafford Rangers in 2005. "I had a fantastic time at Bristol Rovers, and also married my wife while I was down there. And at Shrewsbury Town I'd say I played with one of the best sets of lads I came across during my playing career. But Stafford Rangers offered new opportunities. I could continue playing but also build my coaching and managerial knowledge watching Phil Robinson. Moreover, it was the chance I needed to start my degree in Theology. So the time at Stafford was a real turning point in my life. It was a period of reflection and a chance to do things that had been on hold for years."

With a few niggling injuries starting to slow him down as a player the emphasis on coaching intensified. At the same time, a desire to teach was realised as academic qualifications were achieved. "Teaching is something that appealed to me over a number of years, whether that's out on the pitch or in a classroom. Theology is important to me, but I have started to enjoy history and citizenship studies. That's been great fun, seeing pupils really enjoy learning. I gained teaching experience back in Crewe at King's Grove and St. Thomas More schools, so seeing the reaction of the older kids who remember me as a footballer, has been amusing. Others know me from coaching around the schools. Hopefully, I do enough to impress them and gain respect. That's important for everyone if teaching is to succeed."

In the summer of 2009 the local lad made a full return to the area's football scene with Alex neighbours Nantwich Town. While former Dabbers boss Steve Davis switched to Gresty Road the opportunity to become player/assistant manager to Peter Hall at the impressive Weaver Stadium was too much to resist. "The possibilities at Nantwich Town are endless, but I think it's important to maintain a sense of perspective. A lot of non-league teams think they'll make it but you need to take things steady. I saw enough at Stafford to realise that making the next step up is very difficult, so hopefully I can bring a little experience to the very ambitious people at Nantwich. I'd love to play some more while I'm still fit, but coaching and, maybe, managing is something I'd like to continue for as long as possible. We'll see. Until then, my teaching qualifications are now complete and I'm entering an important phase of my new career. This is likely to be my main income now for my wife and two children, so I need to get my priorities right. The football, however, will always play a big part in my life, and I hope to be involved in some way for many years to come. Whether I'm good enough for management at a decent level remains to be seen. I've had a lot of help and inspiration from my parents, my priest at church, coaches in football and of course from the fans. So I'll be giving it my best shot, as I continue to do as a player..."

Ed Whitby
Made in Crewe

The sound of an ice cream van chime is something that excites children and adults alike. So growing up around the world's leading manufacturer of such bespoke vehicles must have been a dream come true. Ed Whitby helps manage Crewe firm Whitby Morrison, although joining the family business wasn't always the plan…

"I grew up in Haslington, and then moved into Crewe to live with my father in my teens. The whole ice cream thing was an ongoing joke with friends. However, there was always a good selection in the freezer - and they didn't complain about that! The factory was a fascinating place, and I'd always admired my father and grandfather for their achievements, as both were proper engineers. In fact, my grandfather, Bryan, invented a new Direct Drive System that allowed cooling equipment to be powered from the engine. It removed the need to incorporate bulky generators, and set the company apart from similar manufacturers of ice cream mobiles. It is now an industry standard around the world."

Despite Ed's admiration for the family firm's outstanding achievements, his working life started elsewhere. "I wanted to succeed in my own right, so after finishing university I went to work for a wine company in Leeds. About a year later, although I had done well I'd never settled, so I met my dad, Stuart, for a chat. We talked more that night than we had in years, and he revealed that they needed someone in sales. Working with my father hadn't crossed my mind before, and I wasn't really a salesman. Still, he spoke with such passion about the business, and it sounded like the opportunity I had been looking for. My grandfather was delighted when he heard that I was taking the job, while the rest of the family were a little surprised. I had little product knowledge, so I shadowed the main sales guy for several months before joining the shop floor for additional training. That was essential, as I needed to learn every aspect of the business. In a way, I had to prove myself to the people who had worked hard for the firm across many years. There was an incredible pool of valuable expertise to draw upon, so I was able to cover each area of manufacturing. I starting with the fibreglass body, moved on to the refrigeration unit, welding and finalising the van – all real coach building skills. I just got stuck in and gained a sound understanding of the basics, the processes and how the product was made. It also gave people a chance to learn about me."

In late 2007, the factory's production manager decided to move on and another interesting opportunity cropped up. "I'd only been with the business for a few years, so this was a big step. However, while I'd been learning, I had also identified a number of areas that I felt could be improved - for the good of the factory and the employees. This had to be a two-way process, so I was delighted that the workforce embraced some of my suggestions and trusted me. I wasn't trying to make a name for myself; I just wanted things to be more efficient. That acceptance was a huge relief and I knew then that being associated with the family business had been the right decision."

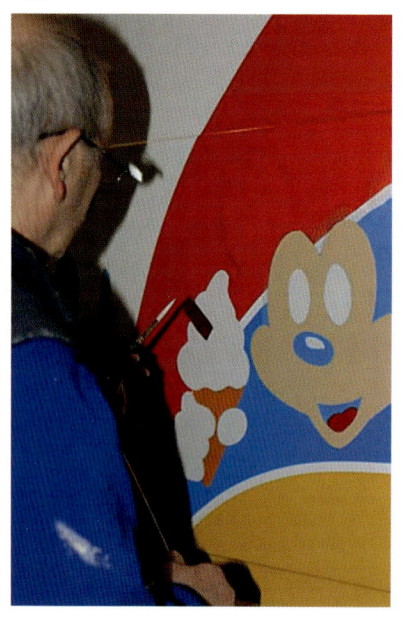

Family connections have played a significant role in the factory's life since the early days when Ed's father made a bold decision himself. "He was an apprentice at Rolls-Royce and became a successful engineer. Then one day he told my grandfather that he wanted to work for the family business. That must have taken guts, leaving a prestigious firm like Royce's, and yet I don't think that our firm would have progressed as it has without him. In a way, that's what I have hoped to achieve – to offer something new and to compliment what was already in place. We all want the same thing; to be successful and professional, but to run a relaxed and friendly company. That, thankfully, is something that has happened across the decades. We now have about fifty people working at the factory, and nearly all of them live in and around the town. There are also three father-son teams around the shop floor. Then there's Dave, our refrigeration engineer and longest serving employee, who started working with my grandfather in 1967. Even the apprentices have stayed loyal. All seven who have joined the business over the last three years are still with us. They even socialise together, so there must be something about the place that helps to create strong bonds."

Increasingly important to the firm is its relationship with the town and other Crewe organisations. "We have a unique product and only sell the occasional vehicle in this area. In reality, we're a global brand, selling all over the world. However, we have had sponsorship packages at Crewe Alexandra since I was a kid, and two employees joined the firm because of adverts they saw in the matchday programme. Then there is the Crewe Heritage Centre, somewhere we can show off some of our vehicles. Our business has been here for a long time and we believe that the end product - the mobiles - should be celebrated, just as locomotives and cars have been at other museums. There's pride in what we do, and we'd like people from the town to share that. The ITV Heartbeat series used one of our vans, as did the Boddington's brewery in one of their adverts. Recently, Nokia approached us wanting to promote their handsets with one of our vehicles. When you're on holiday, people always ask where you come from. We think it would be great if people said Crewe – the place they make ice cream vans."

Media exposure is increasingly important to any company, and Whitby Morrison recently enjoyed the attention of a well-known comedian. "We often get calls about our vans, usually for weddings or surprise birthday parties. So a call from Eddie Izzard's agent was a surprise. I was a little sceptical at first, but it turned out that Eddie was going to run 1000 miles around the UK, for the Sport Relief charity. He wanted an ice cream van instead of a conventional support bus! I thought about it, ran it past my father and talked to a few other people. Dad wasn't sure, but I thought it was a superb opportunity for our company, and also a chance to help a national charity. Eddie's management team clinched it for me when they came to our factory and showed a real interest in our work. They were also happy for us to design the van's colour scheme. So Eddie got a top-of-the-range mobile that would give out free ice cream to people he met around the UK during his epic journey. We all teamed up on the Wirral leg of his tour, and my dad ran with him for a few miles. The challenge ended in Trafalgar Square to incredible media attention. In the background of many interviews was our van. That made me very proud. Our unique product, made in Crewe, by our fantastic team of people on Weston Road."

With such an excellent profile already established, everyone at the factory is hungry for more. "There is new film being made in Crewe in 2010, about a local man starting an American Football team here in the 1980s. That's perfect for us, being able to back a quirky production about the town and see one of our vans in an international movie. The American angle and subsequent distribution in the United States will ensure that a Crewe business is seen around the world. That will link well with our plans to expand sales around the globe. This town has a lot to be proud of, and I hope that we can encourage more people to be positive about Crewe."

Dorothy Flude
A Social Conscience

A childhood memory would affect Dorothy Flude across her working life with social services, a career that allowed her to help improve the lives of others. An unexpected illness forced early retirement, but inadvertently led to council duty. A socialist to the core, representing those around her would always come before political dogma...

"My father's family have been in this area since the 1630s, the Crewe family, farmers from the villages that surround the town. My mother's relations came from Kerry, Montgomeryshire, mid Wales, to work for the London & North-Western Railway. We have always lived and worked in this area. My children were born in Cyprus and we then lived in Germany, at a place called Bergen Belson, near to the concentration camp. So that had a profound effect upon me and ignited a passion to stop people suffering and being treated unfairly."

One incident in early life had a major impact on Dorothy. "I had an uncle who had a learning difficulty. One day, in the 1950s, he was in the town square causing a nuisance. He wasn't hurting anyone, but he was arrested because he was dancing around the war memorial in Market Square. Such places were seen as sacred in the 1950s, and society didn't understand people with learning difficulties. Care in the community was not an option for people like him back then, so the easy option was to lock them away – out of sight, out of mind. He was taken away to a place called Calderstones, in Lancashire, a large Victorian mental hospital on the moors. Most days, they didn't get them dressed unless a visitor rang at the lodge gates asking to see them. It was a long way to travel if the family wanted to see him, so that didn't happen very often. After a lot of campaigning and letters to health officials, my grandmother managed to get him transferred to Cranage Hospital, near Holmes Chapel. Even there it was restricted access, only one visit a month in those days. My uncle spent his life in institutions and never had the opportunities that people who have a learning difficulties have today"

With such memories always playing on her mind, it was no surprise that Dorothy eventually entered a career in social care. "I started at the Hilary Centre on Salisbury Avenue, just down from the old convent. After a few years I qualified and eventually became a manager of several social work teams, occupational therapy teams at day centres and residential homes, facilities for people with learning and physical disabilities. We saw a lot of changes during my time there, and I enjoyed the challenges and have many good memories of the people I worked with. I became very ill and was forced to retire early in 2000, as I had a brain tumour and my world was turned upside down. For the first time, I saw how care services were delivered – but from a patient's perspective!"

Several years of convalescence followed, and Dorothy used some of her time helping out at the Labour Party's HQ on Nantwich Road "It was during Gwyneth Dunwoody's time in office. I helped with the envelopes and did a few admin tasks, but also got to know the local Labour Party members. Then, in 2004, when Crewe South County Councillor Geoff Minshall died, I was put forward to stand for the vacant seat. To my amazement, I was elected. When they split Cheshire East and West I was elected to represent Crewe South, and I also made history when I became the first woman to lead a Labour Group on a council in Cheshire. Most recently, the Charter Trustees made me the Mayor of Crewe Town. That's an honour that I was not expecting. I work to the principal that if I take up a resident's issue, I tell them whether it's possible to make the changes needed. If not, I will always tell them why not."

Sometimes, it has been necessary to take on the party, something that holds no fear for a woman determined to put constituents' wishes first. "Nationally, my government, the Labour Party, decided that they needed to find accommodation for people out on bail or needing a place after prison. They went to a company called ClearSprings to provide the appropriate care and support for these offenders. The contract that ClearSprings had with the government quite clearly stated that they had to consult with residents and the local authorities where bail homes were to be established, but that didn't happen. In my opinion, they came to towns like Crewe and targeted areas where they think that people wouldn't object, and then set up their bail houses. There were two examples locally: Lunt Avenue and Derrington Avenue. Amazingly, the local police didn't know about them! One night, there were problems and things came to a head. People realised that they had not been informed about who was living in their neighbourhood, so I went completely against my government's policy. The hostels were having a detrimental effect on the lives of the people in the ward. That wasn't acceptable, so, with the help of the local residents and the *Crewe Chronicle*, I stuck at it and went to see Jack Straw, the Home Secretary. I told him that we wanted to close the premises, and that the hostels should be located somewhere more suitable. He closed them both. There are times when you have to go against your political party in order to support the needs of the local residents. We need to house ex-offenders, but hostels must be staffed, and placed in the right locality."

At the heart of most decisions made by Dorothy is a strong, socialist ideology that demands a level playing field for all. "My socialist beliefs have always been very important to me. When I was ill, I needed care services, and without the support from my family and friends I would not have survived. My praise for my doctor and the NHS set up by the Labour Government cannot be measured. Good, socialist values go much deeper than that. Everyone needs a home, a decent education, employment and access to health care. That is the only way people can then aspire to better things. If people are deprived, or isolated, they will never prosper. As a councillor, one key area for me is ensuring that proper services are delivered to the people of Crewe. Being able to represent the people of this town is not a job; it's a privilege and an opportunity to empower others."

There is one project, however, that could keep Dorothy busy for some time. "I am passionate about our town's history and I am saddened that so much has been destroyed. Civic pride is very important, and I would like to see some part of the railway works turned into a museum - similar to the exhibition hall at York. Francis Webb's desk, for example, is tucked away in a storeroom at York. That's tragic, and there are hundreds of other mothballed items relating to Crewe that should be available for all to see. We have a wonderful industrial heritage, and there should be the political will and the co-operation of the many history societies and railway groups to make things happen. Fingers crossed…"

Jacqueline Weatherill with Dorothy.

Andy Scoffin
Painting the Town Red

The 1970s provide fond teenage memories of football, speedway and music for one young railwayman. The town's pubs and clubs were his playground, and they would later see him on the decks and behind the microphone providing the entertainment for others. One pub in particular was special, but is no longer standing...

"We moved from Glover Street to Nutfield Avenue while I was still at Primary School, and although I then attended Broad Street Juniors I remember one year when my age group had to go up to North Street Methodist. There wasn't enough room, so I suppose using the church buildings was a simple solution. We didn't mind, as you felt special being the only kids at a different building. There was an old railway carriage at the back of the school, and sometimes we were allowed to play in it. Then I went to Ludford Street, usually cutting through the cemetery as I made my way to school. When the mornings were misty it was a pretty eerie place, although the conker trees were fantastic around there."

During secondary school, two sporting passions developed – speedway and football. "I had ten bob pocket money each week in 1970/71. It was a shilling to get into the Alex and about the same at the speedway. Throw in a couple of programmes, a drink and some sweets and that was soon gone. Dad took me to both in the late sixties, and I often went to the speedway with a family from Marley Avenue. It's funny because the cinder bank at each end of the Alex ground was similar to the speedway track. There, I stood in between the first and second bend and got covered in red dust from the shale that was tossed up and over the barrier every week. Mum went mad and made me wash as soon as I came in. We didn't have a shower in those days and I had long hair, so it was head in the sink with a few pans of cold water!"

The Crewe Kings speedway scene came to an abrupt end in 1975, but something else was already playing a big part in the teenager's life. "The Alex and the Kings dominated for a while but, from about 14, music took over. As a kid I was mad on the Beatles. I just took to them and knew every one of their songs throughout the sixties. Then record collecting took hold of me. You just need to look at the old vinyl record collection I've amassed to understand how it consumed me. What helped was the massive youth club scene in the seventies where other kids were always playing music. That's when I became a DJ. It started when we travelled all over to get into youth clubs, from the All Saints Church on Stewart Street to a small place in Wheelock. We'd go anywhere. It was a great scene. Perhaps my favourite place was the annexe at St. Barnabas Church on West Street. That was my pre-school before I went to West Street Infants. It got really popular, packed every week with a great mix of people from all over town. We pooled our records and managed to get some DJ kit together - double decks, speakers and an amp. We loved it. So four of us started to go on the road and made a few quid. Albert Dean was the main proprietor, a couple of years older than us. He had the best gear! We managed to do a few big gigs, private parties, weddings, receptions and all that. We called ourselves Barney's Disco."

School came to an end but the DJ business

continued, although the lads also entered the real world of work. "I went straight into 'The Works' on an apprenticeship. It was strange because my family weren't railway people, and that usually got you in. So I was lucky. I remember how they paid us in cash each week, in an envelope with a see-through panel. They employed people to fold the notes so that they overlapped and you could see the edge of the fivers and pounds. That was so you could check it without having to open it. One thing you did back then was pay into the British Rail Staff Association. It was only a few pence each week. We twigged early on that membership would get us into the LMR Club - and get us served beer. We got a proper LMR railway card, mauve coloured like the company badge. It was the same at the Permanent Way Club on Gresty Road, and many other clubs based on train stations around the country when we went to Alex away games. It was our ticket in, although we weren't old enough."

There was a massive social scene around the railway clubs, but as the young railway lads became of age they looked for more varied entertainment. "The bingo and cabaret got a bit stale and we started trying a few of the town's drinking holes. One of my favourites was the Rendezvous Club above Burton's tailors, which was a proper ballroom before my time. The dance floor was sprung, so it was superb for Northern Soul that was sweeping the nation at the time. Before that, a big gang of us had a weekend pub circuit, from the Junction opposite the club, up Victoria Street to the old Angel, the Star and then the Burton. The town centre pubs were busy in those days. Over near the football ground was a club called Up The Junction, on South Street. That was a great venue spread over two floors and I had my 21st birthday there. Years later, I'd even celebrate my fiftieth there. It's a pool club now, but still perfect for a few pre-match beers!"

One other pub also stood out for the young railwaymen. "The Chetwode was a great mix of people. The bar was full of darts and domino players, while the lounge was mixed. They also had pool table at the back. It was also a Whitbread's pub, and their beer was popular. I drank Chester's Mild, which was strange for a young kid. But I loved it. So when they announced that the pub was closing I was devastated. I'd built up a large group of friends at the Chetwode and none of us accepted that it had to close, all because they wanted to widen the road. Progress! The campaign to save the pub dragged on for months and we put a big banner on the building next to the old doctor's at the top of West Street. It said 'God Save The Chetwode' and it prompted the vicar from St. Paul's, Colin Aylsbury, to come into the bar one night. We were a bit worried, God fearing I suppose. But he smiled and told us that if it meant that much why didn't we come over to the church that Sunday and ask the big man ourselves! A group of us marched to the Municipal Buildings to register our feelings, but the councillors didn't want to listen. It was a done deal to shut it down. But the last night party was fantastic. The licensing laws were tight in those days, so John Callaghan, the landlord, shut the doors at 11pm and let us carry on. The rumour was that a punter who had been kicked out tipped the police about after hours drinking. The police burst in and kicked everyone out. Unfortunately, they'd clocked a few people handing over money. So a few got arrested and that added to the bad feeling. A few weeks later it was painful watching the old place coming down, roof set on fire, bulldozer moving in. I'll never forgive the council."

Jo Hassan
Keeping the Faith

In the late 1980s Jo Hassan moved to Cheshire for economic reasons and made Crewe her home. Her Christian faith would be tested over subsequent years, but community spirit and one of the churches built by the Grand Junction Railway Company would ensure that her desire to engage with people would never diminish…

"We came from Surrey originally. We couldn't afford housing down there, so our quest to buy a house drove us up north. My husband, Andy, changed his job and we were advised that Warrington was good for employment and cheaper housing, but it just didn't work out and we absolutely hated it. There was no community spirit. So we came to Crewe, initially because of West Street Baptist Church. That was our thinking: find a church and then somewhere to live nearby. Crewe was perfect, and we moved into a five-bedroom, tumbledown house on Heathfield Avenue. It was a real challenge, with so much to do. It had been flats for years and we wanted to restore it to its Victorian glory. What startled us was that we had so many neighbours knocking on the door bringing cakes, casseroles and welcome presents. This was a local community embracing a new family. It was wonderful and we knew then that we'd remain in the town."

With a young, growing family it was also essential that local support groups were on hand. Jo found these on her doorstep in the Hightown area and she soon became active around the community herself. "I went along to the mother and toddler group at both the Methodist and Baptist churches, then the playgroups on Delamere Street and at Victoria School, and eventually got involved with Beechwood Primary School. Everything was just right and we felt as though we belonged. It was such a strong community spirit, more than we had experienced anywhere else. We wanted to give something back so we started going to a house group that brought around 25 people together. It was the only group of its kind in the centre of Crewe, with members from Samuel Street, Richard Moon and Broad Streets. There were some who needed help, support and encouragement, others who just enjoying meeting and chatting. It was a way of people working together and sharing common beliefs."

The warmth of the church congregation and a desire to do even more for the community saw Jo and Andy become heavily involved at West Street Baptist Church. "Within a year we had joined one of the leadership teams. We then ran activities around the Derby Docks, there was a youth group for the 14-18-age range, and the 5-Minus mother and toddler group expanded. Andy also began playing in a newly formed local football team. We were also baptised to show our commitment to Crewe and the church. Things then moved to the streets of Crewe as we started to share love with people not involved with church. There was a mixed reception, but we expected that. Many of the children from church were involved, and people were impressed that they wanted to share their faith. This extended to practical experiences, like gardening, painting and decorating at older people's homes. There was a lot going on and we saw a massive increase in the number of young people involved with the church and what we were doing."

Then things suddenly changed. The drive to involve teenagers wasn't what some of the congregation wanted, and it became apparent that not everyone was comfortable with the new kids' lifestyles. Maybe some people were confused about what we were trying to achieve. Also, the fact that these youngsters had been involved in drugs and petty crime didn't go down well. The demographic of the overall group had changed and this, to some, wasn't acceptable. There was a threat to the safe, middle class values that dominated the church. I loved to see the kids express themselves, be radical and opinionated, but this was obviously a threat to some of the other church members."

Jo, Andy and others held firm but it was obvious that some of the senior members had made a decision - without them. "The leadership told us to back off. They made it very uncomfortable for everyone. The kids involved were distraught and it led to some damage being done to cars and property. It was out of our control and it broke my heart. It was such an upheaval that we decided to move - from the church and the area. We found a house in the north of Crewe but our ties with church disappeared. We entered a wilderness period, and although we had spells attending other churches it didn't feel the same. There were plans to start something in Leighton, a simple meeting place, but it never happened. Our daughters began ballet lessons at Jackie Capper's, eventually joining Beth Portman's Masquerade. Our son started playing football on Sundays, resulting in Andy training to be a FA football coach and managing one of the teams at the Eric Swan sports ground in Wistaston. But it was a frustrating time as we still wanted to be involved spiritually in some way."

A few years later a chance meeting via an Internet faith forum opened new doors. "A guy called Tim Prevett was keen to involve people at St. Andrews and Christ Church. We tried it and soon got involved in Crewe issues again, which felt so good. Years earlier we had made a commitment; we promised ourselves to the town to show our gratitude to those who welcomed us when we arrived. It would have been easy to allow petty differences to drive us away but we always felt that our faith was stronger than that. We just needed a way to express it once again."

Carey Willetts with Jo's girls.

That new outlet came with the introduction of two innovative ideas that would deliver a Christian message to those who felt disenfranchised with old-school church. "We got involved with Sofachurch because it was so relevant to modern-day faith. It offered an informal setting, sofas and coffee, watching films and discussing life's issues. It was aimed at linking people who can't easily relate to traditional church. The focus was on what it is like to have a relationship with God within contemporary society. It was the perfect environment that allowed people to express themselves. A natural progression was to do similar in a day-to-day venue; so another initiative called Cafechurch was launched at Tesco's Costa Coffee. Same idea, but even more accessible, somewhere to sit and chat after shopping."

With a renewed faith, a more formal link was established with one of Crewe's oldest churches. It would be the start of fresh challenges. "Some of the Sofachurch group had links with Christ Church and the more we thought about it we decided that this central location was perfect to move things forward. We're not out to preach but I think it's important that people realise there is someone to talk with, somewhere to think, interact and maybe form friendships. That's what the Christian faith should be about. Historically, Christ Church was always pivotal to the Crewe community that grew up around the early railway works. These days there are few houses nearby, but there are offices and shops. It could be a spiritual drop-in centre, without being too formal. It needs to be open across the week without any of the traditional barriers. Gone are the days when people would willingly turn up on a Sunday, dressed in their best suits and wearing hats. We don't want to enforce Christianity, but we do want to listen and to make people feel welcome. I think that churches and Christians can be seen to have forgotten how to engage with people. We want to change that..."

Andy and Jo at the Cafe Church.

John Rhodes
United We Stand

After 42 years with one company, John Rhodes deserves more than a gold clock. Two long service milestones have been passed, but the Chairman of the Works Committee never planned to retire early. His working life with Rolls-Royce and Bentley Motors has seen him negotiating on behalf of thousands of colleagues...

"As kids we hardly ever left our street. There was the school, corner shops, pubs, a couple of chippies and our house. They knocked it all down in the early 1970s, and a few years later they built an ASDA store. I was born in the front room of number 63 Beech Street, roughly where the small car park is now. My father was a mainline steam train driver, and other family members were signalmen or fitters in 'The Works'. So the natural choice was to follow them. Instead, I picked Royce's because my brother-in-law, Roy, worked there. It was considered to be the best place in town, so I put family links aside and in September 1967 I started as a craft apprentice."

During those early years the preferred mode of transport amongst workers was the bike. This spurned an associated phenomenon unique to towns with large factories. "I've always cycled to work. There's been no excuse to drive, as I've never lived more than two miles away. It was an

Beech Street in the 1960s.

amazing sight in the morning as we peddled along West Street towards the factory. Men rode five abreast, chatting as they cycled. It was bedlam. There weren't many cars in those days, but when shifts knocked off the motorists knew that it was easier to avoid them!"

Once inside the factory, life soon changed for the new starters. "I did well in the training school and chose machine tool fitting, which was maintenance of the factory machines. Moving to the shop floor, the real factory if you like, was an eye opener. My foreman was Reg Hough and the shop steward was Ken Twiss, both tough and experienced men. The first thing Ken asked me was if I was in a union. Before I could reply he handed me a form and told me to fill it in. You had a choice, but everyone knew that you had to join. So I chose the Amalgamated Engineering Union, that looked after craftsmen."

Although new to Rolls-Royce, the young fitter already had an understanding of unions. "The biggest fear for any family man is losing his job, so I always appreciated what unions did for the workers. My father was in the National Union of Railwaymen and he always talked about men standing together. The union was how you found out about things, like working conditions, pay deals etc. These days they have human resources. Years ago the unions transmitted the information that was passed around the workforce. So things were very different and the role of the unions wasn't the same as it is today."

The importance of membership became apparent to John in the early 1970s. "The first drama occurred when I finished my apprenticeship. Within a few months of being made permanent, having served my time, I was laid off. The company was struggling and looking to cut costs. Sadly, for our section, the maintenance teams were easy pickings. It was a real wake-up call for me. Work wasn't guaranteed! Luckily, we were guided through it every step of the way and supported by the union. That's probably when I knew that I wanted to be part of the fight."

The natural progression for John was formal union involvement. "As I became more confident I started to speak out more and have an opinion at meetings. I became a safety rep in the mid-70s and that was a responsible position, feeding back to the shop steward. But you couldn't just walk into a full steward's job, as there was always a pecking order amongst union men. You had to wait for them to step down or retire. Most of the senior men were strong characters, bullies even. This was reflective of the company's management. I bided my time until the right opportunity arose, and it was my colleagues who convinced me to step forward. They told me that I was the best man, and I think that I gained enough respect before I took the job."

The early 1980s were dominated by Margaret Thatcher's determination to break Britain's unions. These changes soon filtered down to the Crewe factory. "Communication with the unions changed as the Conservative government tried to break the power of the unions. As laws changed the company seemed to take advantage. They seemed to target certain people for redundancy and tried to move them out. Very often they were union men, so as these senior figures disappeared the existing stewards took more members under their wings. When I started there were probably over 100 stewards across the shop floor. I'd look after about 25 men in the machine tool area. By the late 80s I was looking after about 100 men!"

Perhaps the biggest flashpoint at Royce's came just before the much-publicised miners strike of 1984. The industrial action brought the Pym's Lane factory to a standstill. "These days you can't take employees off site and just walk out. Legislation is in place to stop that. It was different in the 80s. In October 1983 we walked out for five weeks over pay. The stewards took a decision. There was no ballot. There was a lot of bad feeling bubbling away and it didn't take much to bring it to a head, a catalyst that united the factory floor. Most thought that the action would be over quickly, that we didn't have the resolve to tough it out. Crewe people were considered to be steady Eddie workers, a passive workforce. But I've always said that when Crewe people get riled they do something about it. So we picketed the gates each morning. During the strike we had a show of hands each day to see if the workers wanted to continue. They did, although none of us were getting paid. It was a struggle but we all knew that we had to stick together."

The dispute also had side effects. "The whole of the shop floor joined the action, about 3000 people in all. We had eight people on the official picket line, asking office staff to join and support us. Very few of them stood by us and that's never been forgotten. When you look at Bentley Motors today you'll hear associates talking about the two factories. Much of that goes back to that strike in 1983. We call it the Rolls-Royce snobbery. When you spoke to the ordinary workers they'd tell you that they hated the 'them and us' feeling, the separate canteens and different lunch hours. The strike was resolved when the management agreed to more pay, and better terms and conditions. We all lost money though, but we showed them that we meant business and that we couldn't be pushed about. The divide, however, was never bridged."

These days John has a much different approach to recruiting new members, certainly far removed from the strong arm tactics employed by his early leaders. "Generations today believe that they are well educated and articulate and that they don't need unions - until they have a problem, of course! I'm okay with that, if they don't want to join that's fine. I certainly wouldn't force anyone. But I say it how it is. So I'd tell the people who don't think that unions are needed to sort themselves out when they have a problem. You can't have it both ways."

Bentley's modern production line.

Tim Prevett
The Ghost Whisperer

Studying theology, having an interest in the paranormal and taking visitors around Chester encouraged Tim Prevett to look closer to home and investigate Crewe's historic past. Some spooky research at the town's library would see him develop one of the town's quirkier tourist attractions…

"Education brought me to the Crewe area in July 1996, to complete the last two years of my degree course at Regents Theological College in Nantwich. I rented a house on Timbrell Avenue, so the first few years were spent around the West End. My fascination with Crewe's heritage started when I moved to the St. John's area, around Edleston Road. At the same time, I began organising guided walks to prehistoric sites in The Peak District and around North Wales. Then, a year later, I became a Roman Tour Guide in Chester. I took thousands of visitors on costumed walks around the city, and also helped with the Chester Ghost Walk occasionally. A few years later, one quiet afternoon in the reference section of Crewe Library, I unearthed papers relating to the spirit photography of William Hope and 'The Crewe Circle' group that met in the early 1900s. That was fascinating, but I also found a booklet on Bridget Bostock, who was known as 'The Witch of Coppenhall'. I was astounded that these stories were not common knowledge. I had just won a Cheshire tourism award for my work as a tour guide, so I thought that it was about time that something was launched in Crewe."

The easy option would have been to focus on the railways and create a trail around some of the remaining old buildings (that had already been done for a couple of private bookings, but Tim wanted to reach a wider audience). However, some in-depth research convinced him to follow a more mysterious route. "When I discovered other paranormal stories about Crewe I thought that a ghost walk was possible. Hill Street and Heath Street have a superb feeling to them, with the cobbles, the Market Hall and some subtle lighting all adding to the experience. On a foggy evening it can be particularly dramatic. A number of stories cropped up that mentioned this part of town, as well as weird sightings at some of the pubs. There are also grisly stories of vicious murders nearby and out in the countryside! So I had the makings of a decent tour and I set out to portray Crewe in a positive light, and also showcase some of the compelling history of this great historical town."

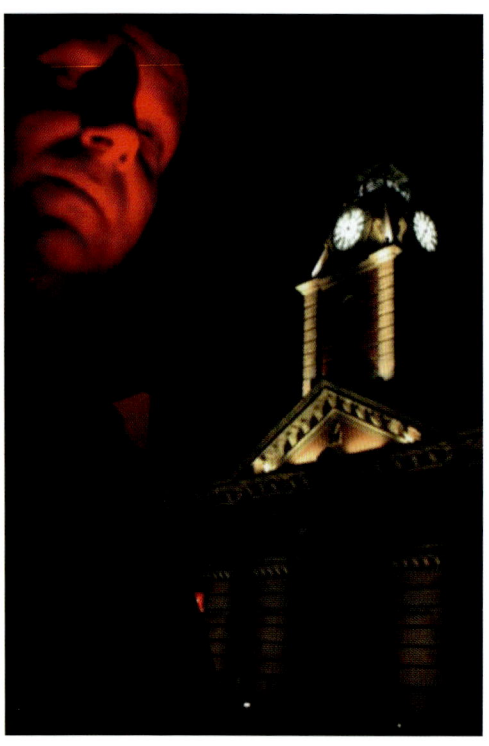

Initial consultations with the council and a number of businesses were positive, and the local media lapped up the story. A few props were acquired, the route mapped out, risk assessments completed and the Crewe Ghost Walk was launched in October 2007. "The day of the first tour around Crewe was crazy. I'd given hundreds of talks to thousands of people over the years, and yet I had butterflies for several hours during the afternoon. The press coverage had been superb and on that opening night two photographers were scheduled to take pictures, so I was incredibly nervous. Around 7pm the first group met on Municipal Square, in the low street lighting that gives the area a mysterious edge. Most of the places had been taken with advance bookings, but a few people arrived without warning to make it a very large group. What grabbed me was the enthusiasm of the visitors. They were delighted that this was happening in Crewe and captivated by what I had to say. I knew that I had the opportunity to establish something truly unique for the town. I had to get it right and build a reputation for consistency and professionalism."

There were, however, a few teething problems. "The inaugural walk opened my eyes to some of today's town centre problems. Just after we set off and headed down the cobbles towards Lyceum Square, a group of about twelve youths started to circle around us. It was intimidating for me, but we moved on and I made sure that subsequent tours stopped by CCTV points. Another stumbling block that night was not having a finishing venue. The tour just ended that first night at the Oak Street car park. So the following morning I spoke with the management at The Three Lamps pub, now called Oscars. They kindly agreed to let me complete the tour at the pub, and to let the visitors into the cellar that backs onto the Lyceum Theatre walls. There are many tales associated with the theatre and a number of people coming on the tour over the following weeks said that they felt 'something' down there.

Word of mouth made that a key feature of the walks. The finish has now transferred to The Heritage Centre (also home to some ghostly encounters) to enable under 18s to join the whole tour."

A number of stop-offs along the walk's route allow visitors to pinpoint people and events from Crewe's history, but two elements of the talk have always enthused Tim. "When I mention the William Hope spirit photography people's eyes light up. From around 1905, extending nearly thirty years, Hope and his associates produced spirit images that captivated the world. Nothing like them had been seen before - ghostly characters appearing behind people, faces in windows and suchlike that couldn't be explained. Many of those photos were staged here in Crewe, so it's another feather in the town's cap, something very different that wouldn't readily be associated with the place. I also love to shock my audience, so I have a number of props that catch them by surprise at different points of the tour. One of my First World War stories involves a sinister raven from Coppenhall, so midway through the tale I produce a bird puppet that squawks as it emerges from my cape, eyes glistening and feathers ruffled. I made a man jump out of his skin one night, then a little girl cried for about ten minutes on another. That was embarrassing, but thankfully her mother thought that it brought the story to life!"

The project has gone from strength to strength and there are big plans for the future. "I have taken over 1000 visitors so far. I branched out to Nantwich in April 2008, attracting many different customers, and I've been delighted to see people trying both experiences. Many come from outside the area, so I hope that I'm doing my bit for local tourism. The town centre tours suit dark evenings, and I want to create another fantastic opportunity. I have already led a one-off walk around Crewe train station's tunnels and I think that Virgin Trains could benefit from some unusual publicity if this could happen more. Travellers with an interest in ghosts and spirits - hidden and haunted heritage - could break their journey at Crewe, even stop over if other tourist attractions emerge. I have strong links with the Heritage Centre and I would love to see them part of a wider group of attractions that make Crewe stand out. Ultimately, I would like to bring in other tour guides just as there are in Chester, effectively creating a varied team. Then someone would always be on hand regardless of my availability…"

A ghostly image of Tim on Hill Street.

Elaine Dodd
Building Bridges in Town

Keeping the town centre vibrant, supporting traders and offering entertainment to shoppers is never easy, but Elaine Dodd enjoyed that challenge for nearly a decade. Moving the war memorial, welcoming Ken Dodd to Crewe and fighting the recession ensured that there was never a dull moment…

"My working life has been with the Council, covering parks administration and then promotion of the Crewe Carnival for many years. I joined the Town Centre Management team just after the millennium celebrations, initially based at the Municipal Buildings. When the Deputy Chief Executive's role disappeared we were moved to the Pyms Lane depot along with other Works teams. That meant we had the people and resources around us to respond to things quickly."

Town Centre Management meant running three very distinct areas of the old borough. "My role covered the centre of Crewe, Nantwich Road and Nantwich town centre - all very different in their own way. There were lots of initiatives ongoing in and around Nantwich and I found that many of the traders were keen to help out. Crewe was very different, and along with assistant Sue Togay (later Jennifer Anderson) we had to work hard to gain their trust. We improved the marketing and encouraged traders to get involved. Retaining footfall was important, as was creating literature that gave customers a reason to visit the shops again. Nantwich is made up of smaller independent traders, who can make decisions quickly as they know their customers and what works for them. Many of the Crewe stores are different, part of regional or national chains. The head office usually holds the purse strings. Also, once trained in Crewe, personnel often move on to other towns or cities, so it's hard to maintain good contacts. As a result, Crewe town centre promotions were often fragmented with some shops not involved."

Attracting new faces to Crewe's shopping core wasn't always the issue, as some existing 'customers' required more attention than others. "A busy town will always encounter problems, especially from shoplifters. So perhaps one of the biggest achievements was launching the SCOOT (Stamp Crime Out Of Town) initiative and being the first Borough in Cheshire to get the Safer Shopping Award. It was a great partnership with Cheshire

Constabulary, in particular Sgt. Nigel Bailey and PC Robert Greig - without whom it wouldn't have happened. The British Retail Consortium also helped to deliver the project plan. That was the start of Crewe town centre networking, and I felt that the local businesses really felt part of it. Eventually, we let go of the reins to Ralph Lewis, ex-manager of Woolworths, and Andrew Carter from Carters Jewellers, so businesses certainly felt more supported with networking from those also in the front line."

"The position was satisfying, too, as you could help people to enjoy the town who might otherwise be excluded. For instance, introducing the Shopmobility scheme to Crewe. Following much lobbying from the Disability Resource Exchange, we acquired some equipment with partnership support and started a temporary operation from a portakabin on the Victoria Car Park next to ASDA. Interestingly, the cabin is still being used some nine years later!"

The new scheme connecting shops via the John Clough Radio Link was particularly useful around Christmas, a stressful but happy time of year for most shoppers. "The lights switch-on was always the highlight of the year. Market Square was packed and we had pantomime characters, Signal Radio, fireworks and a mini fairground. In my last few years we invited Adelaide FM, the local school radio station, to take over the music, and a great young DJ called Chris Gentile became a star. He was superb, and I'll be amazed if he doesn't become a household name in a few years. Including local touches has always made a big difference, like having the Star Search winners also performing on the stage."

A regular visitor to Crewe's Lyceum Theatre was also happy to perform the switch-on, and caused quite a stir one festive period. "Ken Dodd was hilarious when he came to see us. His shows are great but he's just as funny in everyday life. There was still plenty of fuss about his tax evasion trial so he was big news when he arrived in Crewe. While he was here, he cheekily kept asking me to get cracking and make him some Diddy Men! He was always complimentary about the Borough and enjoyed his welcome to the town. He was, however, late everywhere he went because he spoke to every one of his fans! Despite the excitement we tried to create, each year members of the public and a few traders said there were not enough lights. It's all about investment, and as Crewe has much more open space than Nantwich it's hard to make the displays look as effective. You have to balance it against costs and concerns for the environment. So, before I finished, we changed all of the lights to low energy bulbs. We had some great advice from our engineer, Brett Hall and his team who did a fantastic job for the towns. We also secured some cash for new Christmas trees with built-in lights, and some delightful reindeer that look beautiful when lit up. Still, it never seems enough, which is why Nantwich Town Council and a few key traders always like to top up those supplied by the Council."

Addressing lighting issues was a breeze compared to the controversy that surrounded one of the most significant changes to the town centre in many years. "Moving the Britannia War Memorial split the community right down the middle. The town centre staff took plenty of the abuse on a daily basis, often because people didn't have the right information. There was, however, a noticeable difference in attitude between the public and the traders. The business community understood the need to move the memorial, as it was likely to improve the commercial appeal of Market Square. We also worked very closely with the veterans who established a group to assist us, something I don't think the public realised. At the time, Mark Potts and Tony Marks, local historians, provided much of the information for the inscriptions, and they would not have been completed as efficiently without their research and help. The move caused a lot of anguish, but I believe that it was the best solution. Thankfully, the majority now feel that Municipal Square is a credit to the town. We also had staff trained to perform ongoing maintenance on the statue, so she should stay in great condition."

Alongside the memorial switch a new shopping complex was planned. It offered Elaine and the town centre team a fantastic opportunity to put the Crewe shopping experience alongside Chester and Hanley. "It sounded great to start with, but the Modus scheme wasn't destined to happen, especially when the country entered into recession. Crewe needs a major anchor store to attract people in and the other traders need that kind of pull to succeed. It's been a tough time for them, but I'm told there are some revised development plans on the table and I look forward to seeing what might evolve. It would have been exciting to have been part of these new plans."

Delayed developments aside, the bridges built with Crewe and Nantwich traders left Elaine with a real sense of achievement. "Having walked through some doors feeling the need to put a tin hat on, as a Council representative, it became a very close-knit group of people. This happened because of our joint efforts, the involvement and help from many key traders and the support of the local community; it's all to do with teamwork. I developed some great friendships and I managed to introduce many new initiatives that I hope have helped them. I'm still in touch with many of the businesses and groups now and am honoured to call many of them my friends."

Bill Andrew
Life on the Footplate

In the 1950s the sheer scale of steam operations at Crewe was enough to convince Bill Andrew to leave his home town of Burnley. He would go on to drive many fine locomotives the length and breadth of the country, with passengers like Her Majesty The Queen and Harry Potter...

"I joined the Rose Grove steam depot in Burnley when I was fifteen years old. Three years national service interrupted my early working life, and then in 1955 a colleague said he was going to take a look around the North Sheds at Crewe. I wasn't married, so I had nothing to keep me in Lancashire. It was a massive place back then. Two enormous sheds with six lines through each, a roundhouse that could take at least ten locos, plus the outside area where the coaling was done. It stretched from Mill Street over to the Chester line, from the Waverley Court area down to where Wickes DIY store is now. The modern Signalling Centre was built where some of the North Sheds used to stand. When I arrived that day I was speechless. There were Duchesses, Scots and Jubilees everywhere. To me that was heaven. We only had shunters and freight trains at Rose Grove, so my mind was made up immediately. I went home and applied to transfer to Crewe, to be a fireman on some of these magnificent locomotives."

Within six months the move was complete, and Bill joined the team known as 'the extra link'. "I was part of a driver and fireman crew who would book in each day and wait to be allocated a job. Basically, we weren't attached to a regular service. We covered when men were sick or on holidays, plus any additional services that were put on. My first job was covering the ballast train on the Chester Line, firing a steam loco from the South Sheds. Six months in I got my first exciting trip. I was living in the barracks down Gresty Road at the time, what's now part of the YMCA building. The foreman called and told me there was a job heading to London, a double trip that meant stopping over and lodging. This was fantastic - a Scott class, and a long trip on a three-cylinder locomotive. I'd been used to 40-mile trips around Lancashire! The driver that day was a great man called Tacha Baker who'd made hundreds of journeys like this. I fired her up and kept going at a steady pace. After a couple of hours I looked up at Tacha, thinking that we must be

The Stone Yard.

nearly there. He just laughed and said we'd only just gone past Rugby. There was another 80 miles to go! With fourteen coaches and an overall load of 500-plus tonnes it was hard work, non-stop, hardly any time for a breather. You had to get it right, as the driver might need more coal if we hit an incline. So knowing the route was essential, and as a new fireman I relied upon the driver to give me that kind of information."

There was a pecking order amongst crews and promotion happened as and when drivers retired. "The 'links' described the routes that services would take. Number three link would go to Glasgow; number four would cover Manchester, Liverpool and Birmingham etc. I eventually worked my way up to the number two link, which headed north to Perth. That was the premier link that ran from the North Sheds. That was contract mileage, so it was great money, and I managed to buy my first house on Micklewright Avenue for £1200. Those Perth jobs were the cream, and the crews were the kings. My first driver on that route was called Bob Whalley, a short fella, who'd sit on his stool swinging his legs and smoking a pipe as we sped to Scotland with sixteen sleepers behind us. He took it in his stride, a real calming influence. We'd leave Crewe at 10.15pm and the first stop was Motherwell. There were trackside water troughs then, so we went straight through and filled the tanks while we were on the move using the dip scoop. So the hard work was done early in the shift, then it levelled out after that stop. We'd get to Perth around 6.15am, put the engine in the shed, grab a wash and shave, have breakfast and then get to bed in the barracks. I'd grab a full twelve hours sleep, but Bob would be up for lunchtime and enjoying a pint in the club!"

The hectic life of a fireman was fine, but every boy's dream was to drive a steam engine. That happened for Bill in 1963. "In my spare time I started to complete the MIC class - that stood for the Mutual Improvement Class. It was voluntary and took a couple of years, learning the rules, how a locomotive worked and how to drive them. It was a tough course and ended with a three-day exam that tested you on all aspects of the job. I'd grabbed as much knowledge as I could during my time as a fireman, and some of the drivers would let you take the controls while they fired for you. That was unofficial of course, but it gave you hands-on experience. I passed out on steam, but at the same time they were starting to introduce electric locos at Crewe, from the early 1960s. So the next wave of drivers had a lot to learn. Suddenly you had to understand about fuses and circuit breakers. That period saw a lot of men pack it in. It was too much for them, so they went back and worked in the sheds. I carried on with steam for a few years, but then I had to operate the diesels and electrics. It became very confusing in the 1970s, as British Rail awarded contracts to a number of firms, like English Electric, BTH and GEC. They all produced different engines. The intention was to evolve the best, and that's what eventually happened when the class 86 engines arrived. There were a lot of changes as we moved into the 1980s, and by then I'd become a traction inspector. I'd drive them, ride them and liase with the technicians, feeding back any problems or issues that needed to be resolved."

Following privatisation there were many changes of location and name, but Bill's love of driving continued in the background with some of the preserved locomotives at the Crewe Heritage Centre - plus a few special projects. "I've never officially retired. The office work was fine, but I've always loved being on the footplate. When the Queen came here to open the site in 1987 I was in charge of the cavalcade of steam locomotives. One of them, 6201 Princess Elizabeth, which was named after her, is here now. More recently, I was lucky enough to drive the Hogwarts Express in the first four Harry Potter films. They were a great bunch and I made sure I got all of the autographs. During the filming, Robbie Coltrane asked if he could ride the footplate. He got on, did two shovels of coal and realised how hard it was. He was a lovely guy, and as we rolled into Kings Cross he smiled and told me that he was going to try and get down from the engine with dignity. He just about managed it. I'll miss all that, because next February I'm 75 year old. I'm still fit, but I won't be allowed to drive the main line any more. I can still ride the plates, but as I won't have a personal track safety card that will mean I can't get off – unless it's safe in the station somewhere. It's a shame, but when I was at school all I wanted to do was drive a steam train. I've done that and I've had the best of everything."

Peter Kent
Flying the Red Flag

Upholding strong socialist values and serving the Crewe community has featured prominently in Peter Kent's life, as it did for his parents. He has represented the town in many capacities across several decades, and continues to fight for what he believes is best for its people. He would, however, like to silence the moaners!

"I've always considered myself to be a Crewe man, although my mum moved out to Gresty before I was born, to stay with her parents. It was only for a few weeks, as my dad didn't want her to go into labour with the WW2 air raid sirens going off. After that, Newfield Drive was home for most of my early life. Mum and dad were very active in the local Labour Party, both became councillors and they went on to be mayors of the town. So it's no surprise that I had similar beliefs and ambitions. I admired my parents for the work they did on the council, what they stood for and the things they taught me."

His parents' council duties and political beliefs would influence Peter to an extent, but an experience as a child would drive him to fight for people's rights throughout his life. "There were things that I felt very strongly about, especially when they affected the lives of others. From an early age, I was keen to promote more community use of school facilities. After all, the people paid taxes to build these places. As a kid I'd play football on the fields and pitches behind our homes - what would later become Coppenhall School. Suddenly, without warning, Cheshire County Council decided to preserve these fields for the use of the school alone, so they erected a high fence to keep people out. That was open space, our play area as far as we were concerned, so it had a big impact on children in the area. A public facility, shut off to the public - that wasn't right. So that was something that always stayed with me and encouraged me to stand up for people when the system and heavy handed bureaucrats threatened to trample on them."

Although a working life in various railway-related functions beckoned, a commitment to the Labour Party began at fifteen years of age. In fact, it was the start of a memorable period for the Crewe-based socialists. "With some encouragement from my parents, along with a few mates from school, I formed the Labour Party Young Socialists branch in Crewe. We were based on

Heathfield Avenue at the Labour Party HQ, a place called Unity Hall. This was used as a meeting room for party branches, and suddenly there were about 150 young people - aged between 15 and 25 - with record players and table tennis tables causing mayhem. It was effectively a youth club, although there was a core group of people who were interested in serious politics. We used to get at least a dozen going to party conferences, and we made a real impact, flying the flag for Crewe. We were easily the most successful of the young socialist branches across the whole country. Unfortunately, some of the senior figures didn't appreciate this, or the fact that our group had grown so quickly. So we moved to the Co-op Hall by the Ritz, often retiring to the Masonic Arms opposite for post-meeting drinks!"

A councillor from 1971, doing the right thing for the people of Crewe has always been top priority, although the decisions taken have not always been popular. Sometimes, it would also mean standing up to the party. "The Labour-run council of the 1970s had a policy of slum clearance, so a lot of railway cottages disappeared. It wasn't a case of wanting to destroy the town's heritage, but you must realise that a lot of the older councillors had lived through a period when housing conditions were awful. The standard of those buildings was very poor and they wanted to improve the town. Similarly, in 1980, the West Street extension was another example of progress and improvement, but something that angered many local residents. Ultimately, widening the road meant that either the Chetwode Arms or St.

Gordon Brown, Les Wood, Peter, and Gwyneth Dunwoody.

Paul's Church over the road had to be knocked down. I voted against destroying the pub, as did my mother who was also on the council then. We wanted to put the community wishes ahead of the establishment, so I went against the labour whip."

Putting Crewe first has also been very important to Peter, who was the youngest mayor of Crewe & Nantwich Borough Council in 1986. Just four years later, he became the leader of the Labour council and was able to drive key projects forward. "The Wychwood Park development was a bold move as it was on greenbelt land. As a council we were sold on the idea because we genuinely believed that it would benefit Crewe and Nantwich. They talked about new roads, increased use of the station and high-profile golf tournaments. Not all of that happened! Then there was the new warehousing for Gallagher's and their cigarette distribution business. I was against it, as an anti-smoker, but it meant jobs for Crewe. The toughest decision was probably the war memorial move. I had an old lady call me in a very distressed state. She really believed that the memorial contained graves. The hardest part was sticking to our guns, as it was the right decision for the town. The media had whipped up a storm, so it was a messy situation. That's probably why I lost my seat, but the national trend was the reason we lost the council in 2006. On the night of the count I was shocked by the defeat, and yet I wasn't devastated, as some had predicted. Perhaps it was time for me to move on, and that election brought things forward. Too often you have all your party members involved in front line campaigning, running wards or fighting for seats. So helping the local party with its administrative tasks suited me. I've got a lot of satisfaction from that."

With two years taking a back seat, the unexpected death of Crewe and Nantwich MP Gwyneth Dunwoody, in April 2008, shook the Labour Party – locally, and on a national level. It was also a call to rejoin the campaign trail. "Losing Gwyneth was a huge blow, to me and the Labour group. She was godmother to my daughter, Natalie, and someone I considered to be a friend. She was an old-school politician, what I'd call a true parliamentarian.

Her daughter, Tamsin, won the selection contest for the by-election on merit, as she turned in the best performance. However, she was on a hiding to nothing and I felt very sorry for her. I joined her door-to-door canvassing team and also witnessed the campaign around the town. She was let down by senior Labour officials who were not in touch with the town's voters. There were strategic failings on the part of the professional party advisors who effectively ran the campaign, acting on behalf of London. They blew it from the start with the ludicrous 'Tory Toff' campaign. So we lost a seemingly safe Labour seat and, coupled with the decision to change the local government system in the wrong way by lumping us in with Macclesfield and Congleton, I believe that the Labour voice was weakened in this town."

Whatever party flag flies above the constituency, Peter remains passionate about Crewe and improving it for future generations. "The new train station has to happen. It's symbolic, something that is known across the world. Whatever some might think, it's all about the image. Enhancing the look and feel of a town rubs off on its people. Hearts and minds are lifted. We don't celebrate the town enough, and I think that people need to have more pride and not accept second best. No matter what happens I try to remain positive, and if there's one thing I'd like to do it's to string up all the whingers!"

Tamsin Dunwoody campaigning on Nantwich Road.

Wendy Hadaway
Dorothy's Red Shoes

Banger racing, a steady boyfriend and a school bully shaped the life of one fifteen-year-old Crewe girl. Determination and staying power saw her emerge as a strong, confident woman who did everything she set out to achieve. A working mum, she decided to push herself harder and now dreams of graduating in red shoes…

"I grew up with an older brother and a younger sister, on Newfield Drive near the Coppenhall School playing fields. That was our playground until we were old enough to go down to the park off Queen Street. I remember how the field seemed huge when we were kids, and the little play area was the best thing in the world. It's all a bit run down these days. Then, just before I went to secondary school, we moved to Coleridge Way on the Sydney estate. That wasn't a problem as Coppenhall was still the catchment area. So I stayed with my friends and really enjoyed the first years at 'big' school."

Sadly, the arrival of a new girl in year three turned Wendy's world upside down. "She picked on me from day one. I don't think I did anything wrong and yet I was always her target. Maybe I was too soft. But it really affected me. She taunted me every day. So I wagged school a lot of the time. When I was nearly fifteen I started to go and see an older friend who had a flat on Drayton Crescent. We didn't talk about it but I think she knew what was happening. I hated going to school and there wasn't the discipline then to chase up people who didn't attend. So I got away with it and kept clear of my bully. I don't think that mum and dad understood how much it hurt me at first. So I took an overdose to make people sit up and take notice. After that mum insisted that I moved schools. Even now I've blocked out that period of my life, but I went to Kings Grove for my final year, still confused, messed up and emotional, but determined to get through it all."

With such turmoil during her exam period, any careers guidance was vital. The route to an office job was, however, somewhat confused. "We went for a talk about our future one morning. There was an exhibition in the main hall with displays about different types of work. The head teacher asked everyone to pick something, so when I heard someone say 'clerical' I thought I'd go and listen to that presentation, because I wanted to go into the medical profession. I still don't know why, but I was convinced that clerical was connected to the medical world. So I sat listening to a talk about office jobs. Bizarrely, it led to a placement at CHK Engineering, working in the accounts department. That was near to the end of the fifth year and I knew that I wasn't going to pass many exams, so before I left school I started hunting for proper jobs. I figured that if I got work I could think about going back to college. So I saw an advert for an office junior with a solicitor's firm, and I just went for it. They were called Holmes, Hollinshead & Hyatt and were based on Edleston Road at the time, above Moody's jewellery shop. One of the partners seemed to like me, and because I could start after Easter he gave me the job. So I left school on the Friday and started work on the Tuesday after the Bank Holiday. It was only small and the people were fantastic and it was such a change from school. After a few weeks, they sent me on day release to South Cheshire College, studying Business Administration. So things worked out well."

One bright spot during her teenage years was watching the banger racing at the Earle Street stadium. There she met Cliff, a friend of her brother's who helped out with the cars. "We started going to the track just before I left school. Cliff worked at ATS Tyres on Gresty Road and helped out in the pits. The first time I saw him he was filthy and covered in oil, but it was love at first sight. I was usually babysitting my little sister, so it was a while before I got any time alone with Cliff. We eventually started dating, and over twenty years later we're still together, married and with two lovely children - all because of that old speedway track that was eventually pulled down. I miss those days,

Wendy's brother with Cliff at Earle Street.

and I sometimes think of the old stadium when I'm shopping at the retail park that was built in its place."

Although qualifications were thin on the ground, Wendy had always done well at mathematics and typing. As her career at the solicitor's progressed her skills were put to good use. "I remember my dad buying me a typewriter when I was seventeen, and I still have it. That was a great help and because my confidence grew I found that I could achieve things on my own, away from formal education. The partners soon let me loose on the clients, working in reception and then as a secretary. I did well at college and it wasn't long before I was running the accounts." And yet there were challenges on the personal front. "Cliff proposed when I was seventeen and my mum wasn't happy about that. She didn't think we were ready. So I moved in to his mum's house on Frank Webb Avenue. We eventually bought a house on West Street because we could only get a mortgage on Cliff's wage, as I wasn't quite eighteen. That was a massive change for me but it helped to put things into perspective. I knew what I wanted and told Cliff about the milestones I'd like to achieve, like travelling abroad, going to America and Paris, getting married by 21 and having our first baby before I was 25. I achieved them all and I think that added to my confidence."

Wendy and Cliff at The Mals.

Across twenty years Wendy has remained with the same firm, although partners have come and gone, the name has changed and the office has moved to Chantry Court and, most recently, Old Bank Chambers. "The firm has always been good to me and recognised my loyalty and potential. As office manager I have recruited staff, created new companies and restructured the finances. Moving to our current office put us in the heart of town, in a historic Crewe building. That felt good, as I've always loved this town and felt part of it. And yet I have always wanted more, not more from Crewe but more from me. Perhaps because I left school prematurely there has always been a desire to achieve academically. I have always wanted to do my job to the best of my ability, so when my baby girl started pre-school I took the opportunity to enrol at university - in Crewe of course. I've never wanted to leave the town so having MMU Cheshire on the doorstep is fantastic – especially for a mature student. It meant that I could combine work with family and a degree. I could become more efficient and competent at my job, and then give something back to the firm for all they have shown me. This was something I had to do, for myself and also to prove to my kids that anyone can go to university."

With the formal qualification almost a reality, there's one more dream to be fulfilled. "I'd love to graduate in red shoes. Don't ask why, but 'The Wizard of Oz' was a film that stuck with me as a kid. I loved Dorothy's shoes, brash and in your face, and yet if you didn't look down you wouldn't have noticed. I didn't want to be her, but she was a girl that knew what she wanted to be. That's me, just wanting to do what I can without shouting about it."

Wendy with friend Sarah Philpott at MMU.

Mark Potts
Remembering the Fallen

For years Mark Potts relaxed outside work playing football, but a nasty injury encouraged him to take up new interests. A series of in-depth research projects look set to install him as one of Crewe's most prolific writers and a leading authority on the fallen war heroes of Crewe & Nantwich...

"After school I went into Crewe Works, as did many of my friends. The apprenticeship on offer was one of the best around in the 1970s, and everyone had friends or family working somewhere within the sprawling complex that was The Works. It was the natural thing to do. I stayed about nine years and then got itchy feet. I became a Life Assurance salesman but hated every minute of it. The grass was not greener. It just wasn't me and I missed the banter of the factory and the camaraderie. So I went to Rolls-Royce in 1987, long before the Bentley name graced the factory façade."

Around that time, a broken collarbone would inadvertently trigger a lifelong passion: "The war research started when I was forced to break from football. I had been playing in local leagues, even getting a game for Nantwich Town when they were in the North West Counties division. The injury just focused my mind, as I knew that I would need something after football. While I was at home, strapped up and still recovering, a schools programme about the First World War was on TV. The presenter said that every family in Britain knew someone who had died in WW1. The gauntlet was thrown down and I tested the theory on my relatives. My granddad's brother had been killed in France in 1918, so I found out how and where. Amazingly, my father didn't know these facts, or even that his father had lost a brother! So before long I was checking other names on the Crewe and Nantwich memorials, then those in the villages around the borough. I was hooked."

More painstaking research ensued, but within a few years the writing bug demanded more than just facts and figures. A keen film buff, a bizarre subject became the focus of Mark's first book which would also link him with some famous names. "I suppose I was looking for more than a hobby, so I started a project about Laurel & Hardy. I'd watched all of the films but found that I could never get hold of the trivia I needed. So I compiled a compendium, a bible that answered all the questions and identified all of the co-stars from their 106 films together. It was called *What Was The Film When?* I developed good links with Stan Laurel's daughter, Lois, who lives in America, and eventually met her at a Laurel & Hardy convention in Chatham, Kent. The highlight, however, came when I approached Norman Wisdom to write the foreword to the book. Not only did he phone me, he was a delightful man who sent a signed photo with some kind words that complimented the book perfectly."

With his name in print and the debut book well received other topics were considered. But the war theme had played away in the background and couldn't be silenced. Within a couple of years, *Dear Mrs Jones - The Great War Dead of Crewe & Nantwich*, a collaboration with Joy Bratherton, became the first of many war-related works. "Joy ran the local Western Front Association that commemorated everything about WW1 at regular gatherings. Combining my research and Joy's extensive knowledge and contacts we knew that going to print was possible. So we appealed for photos and the finished product emerged in 2001 and sold out within nine months."

Oliver Hardy and Stan Laurel.

Despite being away from research notes and a computer, a chance discovery in France prompted the next title. "I was on holiday with my friend, Tony Marks, celebrating my 40th birthday. We had travelled to Ypres for a few days to visit The Great War battlefields and cemeteries, when we discovered a WW2 grave in a WW1 cemetery. In fact, the name on the headstone was that of a man from Crewe! Tony immediately suggested that we follow up the first *Dear Mrs Jones* book to cover the people who had fallen in WW2. I'd worked hard improving my information over the years, and with Tony's eye for detail the second volume was soon completed."

By 2004 Mark's knowledge of local war dead was so extensive that the borough council commissioned him and close friend Tony to compile a Roll of Honour for the Town Hall. "That was a superb project as the additional backing from the council ensured that we could produce a top quality book that will be on show for years. It filled me with pride that the 1,650 local men and women lost in the two World Wars are now properly recorded, nearly 600 of them with accompanying photos."

Around the same time, a controversial idea to move the Britannia War Memorial from Market Square to the more formal setting of Municipal Square was floated. There was outrage from many veterans, although the memorial was not a war grave. "I didn't take sides at first," recalls Mark, " as I was more interested in getting the names on the memorial correct. So when it became apparent that the memorial would be moved I got involved on the proviso that I could coordinate the creation of new plaques. It was vital that soldiers' names, ranks and regiments were recorded properly."

The much-criticised memorial move took place in 2006 and it was a hectic year for Mark. "Tony and I finished the first *Crewe & Nantwich at War… A Visual Memory* and also updated the Roll of Honour. I also teamed up with Joy again to liase with the memorial contractors before they produced the new plaques. They had to be right. I endured a few sleepless nights leading up to the grand unveiling, and I was there at 7am on the day of the ceremony in Municipal Square!"

In early 2007, Mark and Tony were officially recognised by the Borough when they received a special Mayor's Award for their dedication and hard work. A follow-up edition of *… A Visual Memory* followed and other war themes were hatched. However, it was a wholly different arena that grabbed their attention in mid-2008. "As a kid I was hooked on speedway. The Earle Street stadium was all dirt, noise and the smell of fuel. The buzz of getting up close to the bikes never left me. So with the 40th anniversary of the Crewe Kings' first season almost upon us I knew that I had to document the brief but exciting history. It was also the hardest book I've written, even with three co-authors spreading the load. Tony's attention to detail was vital, while Andy Scoffin and Kevin Tew's speedway expertise were essential."

Lt. Frank Tipping, just one of Mark's 600 local casualty photographs.

Nearly twelve months of toil followed and the book launch was combined with a get-together of riders and supporters at Metz, formerly the Steam nightclub on High Street. Many riders and stadium officials were back in Crewe for the first time since the mid-70s. "Meeting riders who were childhood heroes, men I watched from the stadium terraces, was a real privilege. Phil Crump, John Jackson and Dave Morton made the writing process a pleasure, and it was wonderful discovering how friendly they were, no airs and graces, all of them down to earth blokes who couldn't have been more helpful as we compiled statistics, photos and stories. The launch night was a very special occasion. Events like that make it all worthwhile."

Mark with Kings legend Phil Crump.

David Thomas
The Green Shoots of Hope

A working life maintaining the parks, paths and highways of Crewe eventually led David Thomas back to his childhood playground at Queens Park. It wasn't how he remembered it, but helping to return the old gem to its former glory remains one of his ambitions, something that he's proud to be part of despite a few delays…

"My dad worked on a local branch line railway through North Wales, then got promoted to the mainline with the London Midland and Scottish Railway Company in 1953. So he moved his family to Crewe. He loved working on those old locomotives, but the switch to diesel in the 1960s didn't suit him. He never took to them, and always said that it wasn't like the proper graft he had been used to working the footplate on steam trains. So he joined the Post Office, working with the mail trains. It was physical work, but that's what he'd always known. A few years before I was born, he was unloading mail bags one night when the Scotland to London service stopped at Crewe. He chatted to the driver and some of the crew before they headed off to complete their journey. They never made it, as that was the infamous train that Ronnie Biggs and his gang hijacked."

Like his father, an active, outdoor life was the preferred option for David who left school and headed straight to Reaseheath College. "All I ever wanted to do was work at Queens Park. I spent a lot of time around its grounds as a kid, playing with mates, messing about and chatting to the gardeners. And of course who doesn't remember being chased by the parky for playing football on the grass! It was a beautiful place and everyone talked about it. Working there seemed the perfect way to earn a living, and back then there was a staff of around thirty. But you couldn't just walk into a job, so I took some advice when I left school at 16 and went to Reaseheath to work as a gardener to gain some experience. A guy I worked with for a while left to set up his own business, called Acer, and I decided to join him as a landscape gardener. We covered private gardens and businesses all over Crewe, including big contracts like Air Products on the industrial estate. The business hit hard times so I ended up working for the council in the mid-1980s."

Joining as a gardener/driver, the switch to council work offered some varied challenges around the town. "They had me on tractors to start with, all over the place - cutting grass, moving the planters, watering flower displays in town and replacing the beds. I enjoyed that but a reorganisation meant that I was moved to the highways team. That was very different, heavy lifting, and more structural work on some major projects, like when we replaced the Queensway sewers, paving and road. That was tricky, as the businesses didn't want to be disturbed or lose any trade. So a lot of our work was done after hours or very early in the morning. We laid the block paving from Martin Dawes right down to Perry's fruit shop, where Waterstone's bookshop is now. We'd worked so hard one Sunday that I fell asleep in Perry's doorway when we had finished. The supervisor woke me up with a McDonald's! That wasn't the worst of it. Before we finished the project there was a section that had to be dug up to replace the kerbs. Typically, this was close to electrical cables that ran along Queensway and fed the shops. One morning, around 6.15am, we followed some plans and carefully lifted some kerbs with a digger. Unfortunately, the plans had been copied back to front! We hit a power line and the explosion sounded as though we'd blown up the town centre. The whole place shook. We were told that you could hear the bang over a mile away. It even stopped the Big Bill clock, and it didn't chime properly for three months!"

A company called Jarvis eventually took over the highways contract, and the Crewe workers were allocated positions within the council's maintenance teams. "It made sense for me to return to grounds maintenance. I didn't need to be trained again so I was straight back into it. I started grass cutting, and then working on the new playground installations and maintenance with the Council's engineer. That led to a qualification as a ROSPA inspector, making sure that sites were safe and clean. There were only two of us, so keeping up with the play areas, skate parks and ball courts was a real challenge. I often hear people complaining about the condition of some areas, but it's like painting the Fourth Bridge keeping up with them. The wear and tear is one thing, but the vandalism makes the job almost impossible. The losers are the young kids."

Finally, a permanent move to the town's park team meant that the lad who once lived nearby got his boyhood wish. "I grew up on Ravenscroft Road, within a stone's throw of the old tip and filter beds that later became the municipal golf course behind Queens Park. So much had changed from my early years, and I wonder if the rules, regulations and red tape have spoiled things for children today. It's all about liability now. Fun seems to be a dirty word. When we played at the park there was a slide that was about ten feet high with a wooden box on the top. If you didn't climb on top of that you were a chicken. Everyone knew someone who'd fallen off, broken a bone or been hurt. It was part of growing up, learning about risk and dealing with it. There were also some great attractions to bring people here, like the birds and animals, open-air concerts and the old rowing boats. That's one thing I'd love to see on the lake again. Years ago they used to maintain the boats in a workshop under the band stand. There was even a coal fire down there to keep you warm during winter! During my time I've repaired things like the rocking horse many times. Not only the paintwork, but also the wooden footrest has needed replacing. Little jobs that most visitors don't notice until things are broken or removed."

Since 2006, David and his park colleagues have been in the firing line as a major project to return Queens Park to former Victorian glories has stalled. "It's fair to say that the park has not been kept to the same standard it once was, but you could say the same about most things in life. There's a much smaller team here, doing the same amount of work, and yet plenty of people still enjoy walking around what has remained open. The renovation project hasn't made our jobs any easier and it's been very frustrating working here while half of the park has been out of action. Since the lake was closed and the upper fields were fenced off we have had to answer questions every day. We've become customer service advisors as well as gardeners. If I go out for a drink over the weekend I get people coming up to me asking when the project is going to be finished, so it's clear that the Crewe public is bothered about it. We all want to see it back to its best, and it's been heartbreaking to see the place looking like a building site. We have tried hard to keep what's left looking good. The flowerbeds down the main drive now look fantastic and we have been able to work hard on the shrubs and smaller trees to make sure that they're looking their best. When the park is completed it will be one of the best in the country again. That keeps us going. I just hope that they increase the maintenance team so that it stays that way. The people of Crewe deserve that so that kids growing up want to come and play here, just as I did all those years ago."

David on the Queens Park rocking horse, 1969.

Rob Wykes
The Power of Three

The railways brought Rob Wykes to Crewe in 1994, not to fill one of the conventional engineering roles but as the Railway Chaplain for the North West of England. Then an historic church grabbed his attention and he helped to establish it as a community resource that would offer essential services to the West End of the town...

"I was based at Rail House and my job was to offer spiritual guidance and support to railway people. I also attended incidents that involved railway employees, occasionally visiting families if someone had died. My wife and I were on a very low income and we needed help to establish ourselves in Crewe. So we went to the St. Paul's Centre in Hightown where there was a scheme for people who didn't have much. We managed to get a cooker and a few other things for our home. I took to the place immediately and loved what they were trying to achieve. Then, a couple of years later, the charity trustees invited me to join them. It was called 3C Teamwork at the time, and they were looking for ways to take the venture forward. I joined full-time as the director of pastoral care, with a view to increasing the centre's work within the community. It had been a church until 1984, but over a decade later it was still a vital hub for the Hightown people. I wanted to explore its potential."

As existing personnel moved on the chance to assume overall control presented fresh opportunities. "Around 1997 I became the centre's director and early on I teamed up with a chap called Keith Boughey, who was the Voluntary Section Liaison Officer for Crewe & Nantwich Borough Council. He played a key role in co-ordinating something called the West End Partnership. There was a lot of energy about that team, so I also joined their board and got stuck in. There were some fantastic events being organised, with a real enthusiasm generated around the nearby streets and estates. The West End Carnival was a prime example, and this was separate from the town's main event that took place in late August. We staged it on the King George V playing fields, at the LMR Club and also at the Leighton Centre at the top of Frank Webb Avenue. We had a few floats, stalls and games, plus our mobile disco on the back of a van. It was great seeing so many people getting involved and as a charitable group it was immensely satisfying to think that we were reaching people and making worthwhile connections. Derby

Docks Day was another fun initiative, driven by our relationship with the West Street Baptist Church. A lot of the events had alcohol available, and some of the residents brought drinks along on the day. Sadly, some people abused this privilege and could have spoiled it for the rest. So we focused things on the children more and discouraged the drinking. It worked and there was a much more relaxed atmosphere. These fun days were always free, a way of getting neighbours to come out and chat to each other, and for them to realise that we were there, willing to help."

Events around the community involved many people, but more focused work with needy individuals was vital to progress the centre's core aims. "When I started here it was still 3C Teamwork, but we changed the name to Christian Concern Crewe. We wanted to emphasise what we were all about and remove any ambiguity. We are about Christianity, we are about Crewe and we are about concern for individuals, as simple as that. Back then we were seen as a furniture warehouse for the poor, nothing more. Most people missed the point, that the real beneficiaries were those given opportunities to work within the centre. So it wasn't just about the beds, tables and chairs. One of the guys moving that furniture would be getting his first shot at work in years, learning how to manage a warehouse, building confidence, understanding first aid and developing customer service skills. It was a fantastic opportunity for people who had been long-term unemployed, adults with special needs, people who had been off sick for years and needed to get back into the system. We could provide these chances. This became much easier when Wulvern Housing took over the management of Crewe's council houses. They had more flexibility than the council and were able to enter into many partnerships with organisations such as 3Cs. Many of their tenants now have direct access to our services."

One of the workers at 3Cs.

However, the old church needed to be adapted if such support was to be offered to greater numbers. "I suppose we quickly became a victim of our own success. We knew what we wanted to achieve and yet the facilities were not perfect. We were based in a beautiful old building, carrying on Christian work in a former church, but things had to move with the times. We installed a mezzanine floor around the year 2000 and that gave us some space downstairs. We built a workshop and employed a qualified trainer, a computer suite followed and a room was set aside to offer counselling services – mainly for young, single mothers. The offices were improved and we were able to rent out space to a a number of other charitable organisations. Basically, we share the facilities and offer support to other organisations just as we help individuals. We have had setbacks, and we haven't achieved everything we wanted to - yet. Each year we engage with around 40 people who have specific needs. Those people have different challenges and we tailor the support we give them. Then there are upwards of 400 families who benefit from school clothes, kitchen packs or furniture, and our Friday furniture sale gives hundreds of Crewe families an affordable option. More recently we have engaged with something called Enterprise Coaching. We have a member of staff who is helping to identify how people can start their own businesses. There are parts of the community where unemployment is the norm, but the people still have dreams about setting up on their own. So we have run courses to help people design flyers to start publicising what they hope to achieve, whether that's a window cleaning round, a gardening service or a mobile mechanic."

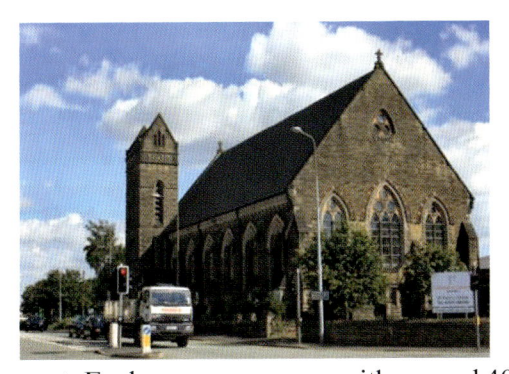

Money, as ever, seems to be the limiting factor, something that stops 3Cs growing as quickly as some might like. "It has been incredibly frustrating trying to attract grants and the rules seem to change as councils and government departments are reorganised. We are lucky in that we own the premises, but we do have a responsibility to the building - and that comes at a cost. It would be easy to sell this plot, for a lot of money, and move elsewhere. But we believe that the heritage is very important, and St. Paul's was a railway church that was paid for by Francis Webb of the LNWR Company. So the roof has been replaced, plumbing and wiring has been upgraded and we have fully compliant access points for people with disabilities. So we've come a long way and the future of 3Cs is very exciting. We're on the edge of the town centre, by one of the large supermarkets and part of the Hightown area that is being redeveloped. There's so much potential here and we want to offer even more to the communities of Crewe. We have big plans to create a café area and to have live music playing, which would be terrific. Our ultimate aim is to branch out and offer our services to a wider audience. That's because I believe that what we do, we do well."

The 3Cs team receiving an award.

Marco Criscuolo
Watching the Cattle Market

Nearly twenty years of commuting from Crewe would take its toll on most travellers, but, when he steps out of the station, Marco Criscuolo still smiles, safe in the knowledge that home is just five minutes walk down Gresty Road. Over the years, he has seen the area change dramatically – the landscape and the people...

"Crewe became home in October 1989 shortly after I'd secured a job in London, as a Customs & Excise Officer. I'd been living in Devon with my father, having returned from several years in Germany. Finding work where I grew up had proved hopeless, so I was looking further afield. Geraldine, my wife, had just given birth to our son, Ruairí, and we were desperate to get our own home. Luckily, her eldest sister, who was based at Leighton Hospital, assured us that the housing up here was more affordable than the South West. She also offered to put us up until we found a place of our own."

Crewe train station would feature heavily over the coming years, and it influenced one of the biggest decisions any family makes. "From the start I was commuting and spending many hours on the trains. I had to work at offices in London and Southend for over a year, before finally making the permanent transfer to Liverpool in February 1991. When that came through we decided to buy a house. Neither of us drives so being close to the station was essential. So Gresty Road was an obvious location – a few minutes walk away, not far from Geraldine's sister and within our budget. When we came to look it over we realised that it was opposite Crewe Alexandra's ground. Behind us was the cattle market, still trading in those days."

What grabbed the new family when they made the former railway terrace their home was the sense of community. "The street was full of families, and people who had lived here for years. Wynn Bailey lived on one side, and she had watched the football club's wooden stand burn down in 1932. On the other side Mrs Jones had been here years. Her husband died in a railway accident and she brought a family up on her own. Then there was Stan, a brickie, and a fella called Ray – both really friendly men. The other houses were full of young families and everyone got to know each other because the kids all played together in the alley at the back. It all started to change in the late nineties. A couple of the older neighbours died or moved to care homes, and it was never the same again. The property boom didn't help, as most of the houses were sold to people who split them into flats. That changed the whole dynamic of the street and the sense of community seemed to disappear. The best experience we've had in many years came when a Polish family moved in next door. They've chatted more than any other new family and we're constantly being given home-cooked food over the fence."

Beyond the alley running behind the Gresty Road terraces was Manley's cattle market. For some time that ensured that nearby streets were bustling when trading took place. "Ruairí's bedroom looked out onto the market. You could see the loading ramp, and every Monday and Friday morning, around 8am, you'd hear the sheep and cattle clattering out of the lorries and into the pens. The noise they generated and the shouts of the farmers and traders were fascinating – unless you were in bed trying to get some sleep! On other days they would bring horses for sale. I took a look one day when they had the Shires on show, and they looked magnificent decked out in their brasses and finery. There was another market across the road past the football ground, but when we arrived most of that had gone. On busy days some of the traders would park up there on the waste ground before they sold it and turned it all into a car park."

The Cattle Market.

The market finally closed and gave way to a modern housing estate, but another historic building also succumbed to the bulldozer around the same time. "Bedford Street School was still standing for a number of years, but the planners said that it had to go in the name of progress. I signed the petition started by local residents, but that had no effect. It was criminal, as there was nothing wrong with the building. Inside were beautiful wooden carvings and staircases, solid wooden floors, big windows and those huge cast iron radiators. They could have done something else with it, but the new housing won the day and they made a token gesture to remember the architecture of the old school. A neighbour told us later that she remembered being marched from Bedford Street down to Pebble Brook School when the changeover happened."

One attraction that has stood the test of time is Crewe Alexandra's modest ground. Just a few years after coming to Crewe, the Criscuolo household witnessed the club's greatest period and the building of a new stand. Marco also wrote a book. "I started writing articles for the fanzine, *Super Dario Land*, in 1993. One piece highlighted some of the club's history and someone suggested that I should find out more. So I started some research, mainly about the origins of the name Alexandra. I found some of the early match reports and decided that the statistics would make a useful database. This went on for over a year and I considered stopping a few times, but Geraldine convinced me to finish it. So I decided to publish it all, with some editorial and a few pictures, and 'Crewe Alexandra – Match by Match' hit the bookshelves in the summer of 1997. That was an amazing time as 'The Alex' had just been promoted. Things got better and better on the pitch, then they announced that the wooden stand was to be replaced, with a massive, modern cantilever structure. It changed our view, but witnessing the work was something I'll never forget. They pulled the old stand down as soon as the final home game finished. The new framework went up in days, and watching the steel workers was amazing. An enormous crane arrived one night and a gang of workers assembled it so that lifting the girders could start first thing in the morning. It was almost like the scenes from the famous New York photos, men walking up and down this structure hundreds of feet in the air. They were fearless. We've also got them to thank for preventing a disaster. One of them came over to the house and told us that our chimney looked unsafe and was about to fall. They were right, and we had it repaired straight away."

Success for the football club continued as they held on to a place in the Championship, but like the neighbourhood around Gresty Road the players became strangers. "Promotion really changed things. As Ruairí grew up he mixed with most of the players' kids, in the bar before and after matches and also popped round to some of their houses. Neil Lennon would cross the road and always say hello if he saw him in the street, and Darren Rowbotham, Marcus Gayle and Dean Greygoose were the friendliest players I met. Then it all stopped. There seemed to be a barrier between fans, players and the club's management. It's as though we were no longer good enough. So if I could have one wish it would be to see that community spirit return here and across the road at the club. I live in hope, because I still love living here."

Marco and friends at the Alex during the mid 90s.

Howard Curran
Time Gentlemen, Please...

Pubs have always been close to Howard Curran's heart, so the demise of the town's drinking holes encouraged him to write a book about the subject. He blames cars, supermarkets, excessive loud music and, to a certain extent, women for their disappearance, but he still manages to enjoy the odd pint when he can...

"My favourite Crewe pub has always been the Hop Pole on Wistaston Road. I grew up in the house next door but one, so its presence and activities were all part of my formative years. It's what I'd call a proper pub, with a lounge, bar, function room, pool, darts and dominoes - and a bowling green at the rear! It's got everything, and unlike many across the town it hasn't tried to reinvent itself. In my younger days, most of them had football and cricket teams, and many would also take part in the local carnival, with the Hop Pole being almost legendary for its participation. Another was the Queens Park Hotel; originally called the Broughton Arms today it's known as The Park. I celebrated my 21st birthday there, when a wonderful lady called Mrs Boffey was in charge. Her family ran a butcher's shop on Mill Street before that, but chose to go into the licensing trade in later life. It suited her, and she was a real character who knew how to handle the customers. The place itself was built by Woolf's, Crewe's one and only beer maker. They had a brewery nearby that used the water from the Valley Brook, or River Waldron if you use its proper name."

Starting as an apprentice in Crewe Works at fifteen meant a few pounds in his pocket and, consequently, the social circuit expanded to include most of the town centre's public houses. "It was very different when I left school. There was no social security or benefits. You went to work, but that also meant you could afford to go out. They were hard times, and an apprentice's wage was little more than a pittance. Still, I enjoyed my life and looked forward to Friday and Saturday nights when friends met up and enjoyed a few beers. We'd start out along our road, and then head towards the Duke of Bridgewater on the crossroads. We'd then turn into what I still call Exchange Street (later renamed Edleston Road) and eventually you'd reach the Commercial, Red Bull and the Adelphi".

"Going the other way, up and over Flag Lane Bridge, you would encounter the Little Vine, then into Victoria Street where there was The Victoria, Burton, Star, Angel Hotel, Swan Hotel (Big Duck) and, finally, the Grand Junction. There was something special about them all, no blasting music in those days, so you could actually talk to each other. You'd pick different pubs on certain nights depending what you wanted to do, or maybe because you wanted to meet up with different people. On our wages it was impossible to drink in them all, but there was certainly plenty of choice."

Home life was also very different, and alcohol was rarely kept in the cupboards. "I don't remember my parents having any drink in the house. However, my father had a quirky drinking habit. When he was ill he'd ask me to nip to the Hop Pole with a jug and get a pint of *'mixed'* for him. Whilst I was away getting the beer he'd put a large poker into the fire. On my return I watched as father plunged the poker into his beer. After a few moments when his beer had 'bubbled' he drank it, with real gusto. When I asked what was that all about, he would reply 'to put some iron into my body'. Other than that, it was just at Christmas when there might be a bottle of sherry, but that would be given to family and friends and would be gone by New Year."

"On odd occasions you'd use a pub's off license sales, and take a bottle home with you - but that was it. There were no supermarkets back then. They've come along later and in my opinion ruined the social life of the local pub. Shopping's easy, but nobody stops to chat. They also allow people to buy packs of cheap beer, with little or no knowledge of where that alcohol will end up. That causes some of the problems we see on our streets today, and it's also seen the demise of many wonderful pubs."

The decline of men-only bars is also something that frustrates Howard, and he feels has probably been a factor in the closure of some pubs. "Women were not allowed in the bar when I was a young man. In fact, very few women even considered venturing into the 'bar' as it was frowned upon. I suppose some would call me a male chauvinist, but along with many others from my era we don't agree with women in the bar. That was for the lads; ladies went in the lounge. That's how it used to be and I think it worked fine. Like it or not, young men often swear. Now I can cuss with the best of them, but it shouldn't be done in front of ladies."

"In Crewe Works bad language was part of everyday working life. But in mixed company it's not really on, that's why I think men and women should have their own sections in a pub. I don't want to offend a lady, and I'm sure a lady doesn't want to be offended by me. That's just the way I was brought up. The bar was sacrosanct for the men. We played dominoes, darts and there was always cheaper beer. It was basic; we didn't want the frills you see in modern bars. It was somewhere you could let go and be free from day-to-day worries. Today's open plan bars leave you with nowhere to escape. That's why I feel lots of men now prefer to get a few cans from the supermarket, and invite a couple of friends round and stay at home."

The bowling green at the Hop Pole.

Many pubs have disappeared since the 'slum clearance' that took place around the central streets of Crewe in the 1960s, but perhaps the most controversial demolition happened in 1980 when Crewe & Nantwich Borough Council pushed through the West Street extension. "The Chetwode Arms was a well-used hostelry that opened its doors in the early 1870s.

Before that it was a farmhouse, but the demands of railway workers saw a lot of public houses appear in the latter part of the nineteenth century. I'm not sure that the council made the right decision about the Chetwode, but they were under pressure to improve the roads at the time. As a nation we got sucked into using cars, and nobody was bothered about global warming or the environment back then. The Council had a tough decision to make. They had to decide whether to knock down the Chetwode or St. Paul's Church opposite. In the end, I think they took the easy option. The daft thing is that within a couple of years the church wasn't being used and became derelict. Thankfully, it was taken over by 3Cs, meaning that at least that building survived the dreaded demolition men."

Another lovely old building under threat is the Earl of Crewe, on Nantwich Road. Once again a supermarket wants to knock something down to build a boring box that will destroy yet more small businesses and pubs. You can't preserve everything, but you must try your best to keep some of the past alive. Pubs are so rich in working class history; they have so many tales to tell and have always been a great place to socialise. It saddens me, but in ten years I think you'll have a job counting twenty pubs in Crewe. That's why I wrote my book, *Crewe Pubs*, to show future generations how the trade once thrived in this industrial town."

Howard with Russ at the Hop Pole.

Ray Bispham
Into the Limelight

From radio engineer to rock club owner, Ray Bispham followed a dream and established one of the best venues in the North West that brought thousands of music fans to Crewe. The club's popularity grew quickly, there were regular sell-out gigs, expansion followed and the BBC made a film about the whole experience…

"Across the 1970s I worked as a radio and TV engineer, gaining some fantastic experience in and around the music industry. I was always a rock fan, so sound checking some of the top acts was a real treat, but ask any music fan and they'll tell you that watching bands is never enough. For me, I always wanted to run gigs and stage successful rock events. I started off at the Cheshire Cheese running a rock disco, then moved to the Earl of Crewe where I hired the upstairs function room. That gave me more control and the numbers grew quickly. People loved the atmosphere, the bands we put on and that a close-knit group of like-minded music lovers could get together in their own space. This was so successful that I started running nights at The Manor, when it was still a proper pub. That was in the late 1980s and early 90s, and I realised that I needed a much bigger venue if the business was to grow. I was still working full-time; at Dane Bank as an electrical technician, then along the tracks servicing telecom equipment for the railways."

Initially looking for a pub with a large back room, a chance discovery set Ray thinking. "The pubs I viewed weren't big enough. The space on offer was no better than the places I'd worked. Then I saw the old church on Hightown. It had operated as the Victoria Snooker Club, but was boarded up. There was a tree growing on the front steps and there was a large For Sale/To Let sign bolted to the wall. It was perfect. I took a look around the place and it was obvious that plenty of work was required, but something felt right about it. You just have a feeling about a place, like a house. So I went for it. Luckily, I had a very clever solicitor and he negotiated a three-year lease that also allowed me to buy the venue, with only inflation added to the original asking price. Then the hard work started!"

Finding a willing workforce was not a problem, as the numerous regulars from Ray's rock nights were keen to see a permanent rock venue open in Crewe. "I was shocked and flattered by the fantastic volunteers who stepped forward to help create the new club. We signed the papers in March 1994 and it took eight months to refurbish the place. I didn't want a lick of paint and a new carpet; it had to be right. So to have plumbers, electricians, plasterers and carpenters offer to help was a humbling experience. It made me realise that Crewe needed a big stage. So we made the best of what we had, as there wasn't a blank chequebook. The Manor was being turned into a food pub, so we bought a lot of the fixtures and fittings from there. Then I heard about a 40-foot bar being sold by Gorsty Hall. We had that delivered by articulated lorry, and it took ten of us to lift it into place. So we opened, finally, in November 1994 on the back of word-of-mouth and some fantastic coverage in the local press. The Limelight was born."

To say the new club flourished is an understatement, but for over a year the band room failed to sell out. "It was a huge success from day one. The main bar and band room were buzzing, but getting that elusive 400 downstairs proved tricky. Then, just over a year after we opened, a local band called Tower Struck Down headlined. They'd played across the country and enjoyed some chart success. I knew it would be a decent crowd but what happened that night took me by surprise. The place filled within 20 minutes of the doors opening. We had people upstairs trying to listen because the band room was full. I knew then that we could make a real success of the place. The Limelight was on the map and, typically, we sold out for a second time the next evening!"

By 1996 the rock formula was well established, but the better cover bands were also attracting large audiences – some of them selling out. "Tribute acts were the natural progression for us. We always had live, local acts on when we could, but the demand for U2, Floyd and Thin Lizzy was phenomenal. We couldn't expect our regulars to watch the same bands again and again, so we started to invite the best of the tribute circuit. Some of them were fantastic, almost the real thing, but at a fraction of the cost. That's what clinched it. Rock fans could go to Liverpool and Manchester, but that would cost £10 on the train, plus £20 to see a band. At the Limelight we could have Australian Pink Floyd, T-Rextasy, Achtung Baby and Limehouse Lizzy on stage for a fiver. The public loved it, and not just the people of Crewe. They came from all over. It was a rock monster growing beyond all expectations."

The Limelight grew steadily, creating the Annexe Bar and, later, buying the adjacent shops that would become the Café Bar. "A lot of the gigs were over subscribed. We'd put Sold Out signs on the door but they still came into the club. So we needed more room. The Annexe would often serve as a spillover space for people who could not get downstairs. We considered extensions and even relocation. It never stopped growing. At one point there was a waiting list for bands to appear at the club, as we just couldn't book them in. It was a crazy journey and I never believed that it would be as successful as it ultimately was. The email list topped 10,000 at its peak and we had 55 staff on the books. It was an enormous family of music fans, people who wanted to be part of a scene. Local businesses used to contact us trying to co-ordinate with gig schedules. When we had big acts on, the local B&Bs would fill up and, sometimes, you couldn't get a room in Crewe because of the bands we had on at the club. I honestly never expected it to be so successful."

Then, seemingly out of the blue in 2007, Ray put the club up for sale. "I don't think people realised how the club had affected me. I was drained. I'm a hands-on kind of guy and I like to be involved from start to finish. So after 14 years I was knackered. It was a tough job and although the club ran like clockwork there was a lot going on behind the scenes. I decided to sell because my doctor told me to take a break. I was seriously stressed out and I needed to step back. The weird thing was that the BBC came to make a film, called 'Into The Limelight', when I decided to sell. So I did a PR job for the incoming buyer, talking about the good times and how much potential The Limelight had. It felt strange, but I wanted to see the venue go from strength to strength. It just needed a new leader. So I'm glad I sold the place, but I do miss it. I've taken The Jolly Tar pub in Wardle and everything is more relaxed. We only have a few staff, we don't have to handle bands that bring three vanloads of equipment, and yet there's a great vibe starting to build. Who knows what will happen in the future..."

The Limelight seen from Jubilee Gardens.

John Fleet
Mr Crewe Alexandra

From ball boy to part-time player, youth coach to kit man, John Fleet knows The Alex inside out. Associated with the club for over half a century, he has played against Brian Clough, made two trips to Wembley and broken the Cheshire Senior Cup! There have been fall-outs, but he still loves the banter with the players...

"The old Cooke's garage was home in the early days, a flat above the showroom off Nantwich Road. I spent most of my time with a mate called Glyn Morris, knocking around the streets near to the Crewe Alex ground. Everything we did involved football, and there was a rough pitch behind the wooden stand that served as our playground. Lads from Gresty Road, Catherine Street, Bedford Street and Claughton Avenue all played there, often with Frank Blunstone and other members of his family. He was a proper Crewe man and loved this club. Even when he became famous he still came to visit, and he always said hello to us. We were a couple of ruffians, and we'd sneak through the fencing to see The Alex games. When they had officials on the lookout, we'd wait until 20 minutes from time when they'd open the gates. When we were ten we became ball boys, and we also earned a few pennies for collecting the teacups at half time. You get bits of plastic these days, but back then it was a decent piece of pottery!"

Modern football stadia are clean and safe, but it was very different in the early 1960s, especially in the lower leagues. "The visit of Tottenham Hotspur in January 1960 was a magic occasion. There were 20,000 people in the ground that day – officially! You couldn't move. Looking back it wasn't safe, but that didn't matter to us. We just retrieved the balls that went over the stands or got stuck on the Gresty Road roof. The club only had two or three match balls in those days, so if one went out of the ground you had to get it back. Some got stuck behind the advertising boards that were bolted to the front of the roof. So we'd shin up the drainpipes, not a care for health and safety, and we could have fallen through that corrugated roof! We just did as we were told, and the crowd always shouted at you as you threw the ball back. It was brilliant. Then we started doing other jobs, like sweeping up, collecting kits for home and reserve games and pushing the wicker baskets of kit, towels and balls down to the train station when the team played away. We had to roll a massive container down the platform and load it on the carriage for the players and staff. They didn't use coaches in those days, and always caught the train. Crewe was perfect for that. We even had to lock up when we got back to the ground, despite being just twelve years old. We got paid two shillings each week for two or three sessions of hard work. They were the best, carefree times of my life."

Football was in John's blood, and at fifteen he joined his lifelong friend Glyn and signed semi-professional forms for his hometown club. "We started in the 'A' team that ran in those days, competing in the Cheshire League and later the North Regional League. My claim to fame was playing against Brian Clough. He'd been injured and was trying to get back to fitness for Middlesbrough, before he left to join Sunderland. It was a Tuesday night, up at the old Ayresome Park ground. He was a great player - tough but fair. Even then, still recovering from an operation, he stood out as a class player. He was the kind of man that inspired you, and I gained good experience from games like that. I also played in the Cheshire Bowl, a competition for The Alex, Stockport County, Tranmere Rovers and Chester. It was a tournament played at the end of the season, and clubs used those games to blood the younger players. So we got some competitive action and played in front of some decent crowds."

Some bad news then halted any professional ambitions, but ensured that John earned a living. "I played football for the club until my early twenties, but they told me I wasn't going to make the first team. The manager, Harry Ware, was good enough to be honest with us. My dad had always wanted me to get a trade, so I'd already started in the printing trade, working at McCorquodale's down Catherine Street. So things worked out well for me, earning a decent wage and a few extra quid still playing part-time for The Alex. You could do that in those days, as the regulations were not as tight. You didn't need to be signed on to get a game. If they needed you, then you could play. Soon after that I tried my luck at Port Vale. I didn't make it, but you had to give it a go, as there was a real hunger to be a player. These days, I think a lot of that determination has gone. So as I got older I started to play in the local leagues. I had a lot of success but I always missed the better standard with The Alex."

The desire to be involved never diminished and it wasn't long before a role cropped up at the club. "I started working with Pat Slack in 1979, helping to run the 'A' team and an emerging youth team. The young lads were the better players from the town, ones that hadn't been picked up by anyone. There wasn't a big scouting network then, so keeping the local lads was easier. So I started to develop a youth team on Tuesday and Thursday nights. One of those lads was Clive Jackson, now the Nantwich Town director. He was a decent player, but his temperament let him down. Let's just say he was in the referee's book more than not! When Dario Gradi came in 1983 we started to structure things more. There was no magic wand, but everyone realised that progress was being made. There was a good atmosphere around the place for the first time in years. We could tell something positive was happening."

The transformation was beyond all expectations, with high-profile player sales, promotions and trips to Wembley over the next decade. "By 1993 I was full time, and I took over from Horace Masser managing the kits and running some of the matchday preparations. We seemed to progress each year, and every season was exciting. Wembley '97 has to be the highlight, as I'm sure many people say. Standing on the edge of that historic pitch, glorious sunshine, watching the final minutes tick by before the referee blew his whistle and we all ran on to celebrate with the players. It meant so much to them, especially lads like Steve Macauley and the goal scorer Shaun Smith. They were real pros that battled for a place from the non-league, so I could relate to them. They never gave in. A few years later they were worthy of their testimonials, and it was a real privilege working with them. Others were a great laugh, like Colin Cramb who was possibly the funniest man in football. Once, in the dressing room before a league game away at Grimsby, he got a piece of white sticky tape and changed one of the letters on Kenny Lunt's shirt. I don't have to spell it out! So Lunty played 90 minutes with that on his back and went berserk after the match. Cramby was just wetting himself as usual. Sometimes, I made them laugh. After we won the Cheshire Senior Cup final at Northwich in 2003, one of the officials handed me the beautiful silver trophy to carry back to the coach, and said to be careful with it, as it had just been insured for £100,000. It was like the European Cup, massive. I stumbled, dropped the lid, and the player that was fixed to the top snapped off. They were doubled up while I hastily got some Super Glue to fix it. Nobody ever noticed, so no harm done!"

Fun and games with Shaun Smith and Steve Macauley.

Paul Ancell
The Council Guy

An outsider who came to Crewe with the task of making important civic decisions, Paul Ancell experienced success, disappointment and frustration in equal measures. His time with Crewe & Nantwich Borough Council came to an end in 2009 with the arrival of a new authority, but he has fond memories and high hopes for the town's future…

"There were mixed feelings as I prepared to leave the role, as I had developed a real affection for Crewe in particular. I came here in 2002, and what has always struck me is the spirit that exists in Crewe, more so than some of the surrounding area. First impressions aren't always great, and when I came here to join the council, people raised eyebrows and wondered what I was doing. Still, as a place to work I'd say it's the best I have known. That's because of the friendly people and their down-to-earth attitude. There's a no-nonsense approach adopted by most, not only around the council but also amongst the businesses, schools and factories. To me that was very refreshing. I always knew where I stood, as people told me exactly what they thought."

One significant change that occurred soon after Paul arrived was the handover of council housing stock to Wulvern Housing. As Chief Planning Officer, this created many challenges. "There was considerable apprehension as we moved to the new arrangement. There had been a lot of planning, and in theory the transition should have been seamless. That, however, is rarely the case. From depending on a team of council officers one day, to forming new relationships with a fresh organisation the next was always likely to be a challenge. For better or worse it's something that has happened across large parts of the country. We are where we are. There were difficult times in the first couple of years, but Wulvern soon found its feet. I believe that it's taking the rights decisions and getting on with fundraising to allow for future investments, perhaps creating the developments of the future that a conventional council would not be able to deliver. Some great partnerships have already been developed, and their fresh approach to housing management can only be good for the 15,000 people in and around Crewe who depend upon their services. I like the organisation and I think that councils running housing is a thing of the past. It is management speak, but Wulvern can work outside the box where councils cannot."

Perhaps the most controversial civic decision in recent times involved the Britannia War memorial. A move from Market Square to Municipal Square coincided with Paul's appointment as Chief Executive of Crewe and Nantwich Borough Council, in 2006. "I was privileged to attend the first Remembrance Day service after the square had been transformed and the war memorial had moved to its new resting place. It had been a traumatic time for the council and the people of the town, as there was widespread animosity fuelled by the campaign to stop the move. Many of the council officers suffered, and I was involved in the lead-up to the move and I've still got the bruises to show for it!

There was a lot of bad feeing and, for some, there still is. However, I genuinely believe that it was the right decision. Moving any memorial is sensitive, and I wouldn't say for one minute that the whole process was handled correctly, but the council learned a lot of lessons along the way. We should have consulted more, listened and involved the public, but the council had the guts to go for it. Then, on that November morning, the sun was glistening off the memorial, thousands of people gathered and positioned themselves at different levels all around the new square. It was a wonderful occasion and I hope that even those opposed to the move could see the real benefits. It's a stunning setting, something everyone in Crewe can be proud about."

Further change was just over the horizon, and it would have consequences for the Chief Executive and the old borough itself. "The announcement that the Crewe and Nantwich Borough Council would disappear came as a huge shock initially. Nobody expected that to be pushed through by the ministers. When it became apparent that I wouldn't be part of the new authority I was effectively out of the loop. We fought the decision initially, but then we had to embrace it and start working towards the future, for the good of the area. Cheshire East is a great area, and there is plenty of potential for growth. I've lived and worked around Cheshire for years, so I'm very confident about the future. Crewe should do well, although in the build-up to the launch of the new authority I don't think that Crewe had a fair crack of the whip. Macclesfield certainly dominated the early proceedings, but even those from the wider area soon started to see the potential of this powerhouse town. There's no conspiracy; Crewe will, I am sure, emerge as a key player within the new authority. At the end of the process, just before handover, there was even a light-hearted moment. We decided to bury a time capsule to commemorate the Council's 35 years, and in the rush to create a suitable chamber by the main entrance the guys drilled straight through to the cellar! That was hastily repaired to spare blushes, but it was better to find out then than when the mayor lowered the box into the hole!"

Day-to-day administration of the town often meant meetings behind closed doors, but one period that saw Crewe's corridors of power in the national spotlight was the May 2008 by-election. "It was both memorable and bizarre. We all wondered how the media would deal with Crewe, and

I thought they might be a bit harsh. In the end, I think the town came out of it quite well and the whole country realised the importance of the result. If anything, the power shift to the Conservatives could also spark further change for the town. One of my biggest regrets was witnessing the Crewe Rail gateway project stall. There always seemed to be obstacles, but if the formidable Gwyneth Dunwoody couldn't get things changed during her time, well, I'd challenge anyone to do better. We kept chipping away, but there were several bodies, funding groups and organisations involved, and quite rightly there needed to be extensive consultation. Less of a regret, although it will happen, is that the shopping core of Crewe hasn't been improved since the late 1970s and early 1980s. There have been big plans, grand ideas and yet the rebuilding work didn't get started during my time. I would have loved to sign off with a stunning transformation under my administrative belt, but it will happen one day."

The final spell could have been more productive under different economic circumstances, but one council guy remains positive about the future. "If I was part of the new authority I would be very positive about Crewe. There is so much scope and potential for growth, I can't see it losing its dominant position in the area. And when it does get the full attention it deserves, to the town centre, the railway station and improved leisure facilities, it will be magnificent. The model town, which many spoke about over a century ago, has changed radically. On the horizon, however, there is potential for something spectacular, something that even Francis Webb would have admired…"

Paul's last day as Chief Executive.

Glynne Henshall
Preserving the Railway Heritage

Her Majesty The Queen prevented Glynne Henshall from attending the grand opening of Crewe's Heritage Centre, but he soon developed an affinity for the place. He would become a regular working volunteer, and over twenty two years later he's still keen to preserve the town's railway past...

"The railways have always been a part of my life. I started school at Pedley Street, which was a railway building, before they moved us to the Hungerford Road School. Then my teenage years were spent at one of the town's older education establishments, Crewe Grammar School which is now Ruskin Sports College. Like many lads I then went straight into 'The Works' in 1980 and completed a four-year apprenticeship. We spent a lot of time in the training classrooms by the Chester Line. It was a good grounding, and I've never looked back."

A few years after he completed his training, the town's Heritage Centre was opened. Glynne, however, missed the official launch because of a special guest at Crewe Works. "When the new centre opened I was at work, but we still got to meet The Queen. She came into 'The Works' to inspect the new locomotives that were being built. The team that had co-ordinated the open day a few weeks earlier, which kicked off the heritage festival, were presented to Her Majesty, although we didn't get to say hello. So because I was busy at work I didn't get to see the exhibition for a couple of weeks. Eventually, I came down to help with Brian Metcalfe's model railway – and I've been here ever since. I began running the model displays and telling visitors about the engines and scenes that had been built. It was an impressive plot, and there was a lot more space when it all opened - including the land where the supermarket now stands. The main exhibition hall looked permanent when it was constructed, but they told us that it was only intended to be an eight-week project. It was just a celebration to mark Crewe's 150th birthday. That's become a running joke, especially when we've repaired things around the site. We always tell each other not to worry because it's only here for a few more weeks!"

Funding is always an issue for charitable organisations, but because of confusion about the centre's lifespan it remained unclear how the management would sustain operations over a longer period. "Everything about that first year was temporary, so I didn't think beyond 1987. I just enjoyed helping out. When it did continue, there were only a handful of volunteers involved. The council had employed several staff during the early years, and then a trust assumed control. However, it soon became clear that money was tight. So it would be good to have more financial support, but a number of other factors have made things awkward. We had a workshop built with some of the cash we received from the sale of the supermarket land, but we have never had full access to that facility. A private engineering organisation started renting it and that generated a small income for us, but it also meant that we couldn't apply for other grants because there was a commercial operation on site. Their involvement works two ways. It can provide some great display items when they are completing work on locomotives, carriages and other vehicles, but it also means that we cannot utilise the workshop fully ourselves. Also, because of health and safety issues, it makes it very difficult to bring school children around the centre during the week."

Once labelled 'The Railway Age', the Heritage Centre is, seemingly, in the ideal position, but there have also been limitations. "The location is great because it's next to the station, on former railway land and also handy for the town centre. However, because of the rail lines, road and the supermarket, expansion has always been difficult. We didn't know about Safeway (now Tesco) to start with, as that was a deal done by the council a couple of years after we opened. It's helped in some ways, as visitors can use the large car park on busy open days, and I suppose we attract a few people who also come here to shop. Unfortunately, it left us without much space, and if you're bringing large locomotives to be restored and displayed you need somewhere much bigger than our existing site. So there have been many discussions over the years about whether we should look for somewhere else, perhaps further down the tracks where other old Crewe Works land is available. As usual, anything like that would cost thousands of pounds, money a charitable organisation like us does not have. We have always had ideas and plans, and when the land was split we did get some money. Unfortunately, too much of that was spent on designs that never came to fruition."

Politics and administrative hassles aside, there have been some exciting projects undertaken by The Heritage Centre team. "A lot of locomotives have been brought here, and engines like the class 47 that we have on site, number D1842, which was the first to be preserved. It was Crewe-built, and that's the reason this centre is here. Working on engines like that maintains a connection with the past, and it certainly sets it apart from other projects. Then around 1991 there was Robert, the first steam engine to be restored in Crewe after Oliver Cromwell was in 1967. There are some Crewe locos over at the National Rail Museum in York, but that's not a problem as some suggest. York already had a tourist industry when they were looking for a national centre, although I believe that Crewe was discussed many years ago. They probably talked about this plot, before it was cleared in the early 1980s. There was a collection at Clapham in London originally, plus several other sites around the country. So they wanted to bring it all together, and York was chosen. They have been good to us, so there's no jealousy. In fact, they have so many exhibits behind the scenes that they would willingly loan us enough to fill an exhibition hall here if we had the space. Again, that's all about money. There's an ongoing dialogue and if we need something they will usually supply it. Maybe we'll get some more space if a mystery benefactor steps forward!"

The ongoing concern remains visitor numbers and how to attract more people to the centre. "A lot of volunteers put some seriously hard work into this place. We always need more, and I'd like to see younger people getting involved, hopefully bringing fresh ideas with them. What we need is to get more people through the doors at weekends and at our special events, as that's our main source of income. The dilemma for the centre's team is how often to refresh the exhibition items. Would regular changes encourage the same people to come more than once each year? What we have done is form relationships with other Crewe organisations, like Bentley Motors, Whitby Morrison and Mornflake Oats. With a wider range of exhibits we will hopefully appeal to a wider cross section of people. It's difficult at times remaining positive, but I must enjoy it as I keep coming back. There's a few years left in me yet, at Bombardier or elsewhere, but even when I retire I'm sure I'll still be helping to preserve Crewe's heritage. There's a core of about 15 volunteers busy on projects and keeping the place running. Whatever the future holds I hope they are all treated properly. It's important that we keep the centre going for the kids who will grow up with no understanding of the railways and what they did for Crewe across the years."

Crewe Heritage Centre.

Dave Preece
A Potted History

Growing up in a pub gave Dave Preece the chance to shoot pool behind closed doors. What most treat as a hobby soon became an obsession for the teenager, made him a few quid and brought international honours. He's played with the best for England, and he opened a pool club in Crewe…

"I was about four years old when I started playing pool, as soon as I was able to hold a cue. That was on my dad's table at his pub, the Old Vine, on Flag Lane by the bridge. I always described it as the Rovers Return of Crewe where you knew everybody else's business. There were some great characters in there, like Paddy the coalman. He was always black, covered in coal dust. Then one day he came in, washed and scrubbed with lovely silver hair. Nobody recognised him! There was Steve, the bin man, who could sup ale for England, and some really funny guys like Jim Evans, a Scouser, and Steve Willet who sometimes worked at the pub. Still, it wasn't until I was about 13 years old when my mum and dad let me play in the pub when it was open to customers – usually on Sunday afternoons and, sometimes, if I'd behaved, on a Saturday night. I played for a team with dad and my brother, Mick. They were the main reason that it was such a respected pool pub, as both had been successful in the local area for years. I got a chance because they played friendly games of doubles at the end of the match, called 'The Gallon'. They don't do that nowadays, but it was a great way of giving your reserves a run-out if they were not old enough or good enough to play for the first team."

Perhaps the youngest player in the pub, Dave soon took on the locals and was topping up his pocket money. "I started beating a few people on Saturday nights and even played for the odd 50p here and there. I improved quickly and played my first competition game for the Old Vine in 1988, aged just 14. I lost to a guy called Keith Fulham - or Fudge, as many locals knew him. Soon after, I was beating my dad and brother regularly. They didn't say much, but deep down I know they were proud that I'd improved my game. Others, like Dave Mason, were true gents. Even though I'd beaten him a few times and maybe caused some embarrassment, he'd always wish me all the best. That taught me how to conduct myself at matches."

Then, at just 16, came the major breakthrough. "After 18 months, playing week-in, week-out for the Old Vine 'A' team, and playing in a few competitions at the pub, I entered my first Crewe Championships. It was, and still is, the most prestigious competition in the area. I'd just celebrated my sixteenth birthday in

Dave at the Vine.

January 1990 and I found myself in the quarter-finals. It was a crazy journey, playing against some legends on the local circuit, and I was wondering how the hell I got there? When I reached the semi-finals I'd made it through from 190 entrants. My semi-final opponent was my hero at the time, Andy Mellor, from the Ashbank pub on Pyms Lane. He was the reigning champion, undefeated in the League for about 40 games spanning about 18 months. Best of three, at 1-1 the nerves got to me. I was shaking like a leaf. When the black finally dropped I almost fainted. I was in the final, staged at the Captain Webb pub on Underwood Lane, against Sean Bartley from the Flying Lady. My dad and Mick came to watch, and the pub was packed. I think the crowd wanted an upset, to see a youth beating one of the big guns. They weren't disappointed. I'd grown in confidence and believed in myself. The match played out like the semi final. All square and down to the last game. I took a shot at the black, a fine cut, and then watched the ball drop as the white travelled around the table and came to rest in a safe spot. I was delighted, the youngest ever winner – a record that stands twenty years later. My dad and our Mick were very proud of me."

The logical progression for the local champion was to move up to county level. That he did, but the leap onto the international circuit came much quicker than anyone expected. "I picked up a few more trophies and did well enough at county level that a guy called Neil Kershaw called me and asked if I fancied joining the International Pool Tour. I did, and within two years I was ranked number 64 in the world. I was then asked if I'd like to turn pro. I jumped at the chance and embarked on a whirlwind tour of games and competitions. It was a crazy few years, hard work and you made sacrifices, but I was ranked number 33 by the year 2000. It was a great feeling, but for all of the trips and fancy tournaments I always wanted to do something back in Crewe."

Dave's dream came true in 2005 when his wife, Jen, suggested opening his own pool club. "It was a busy year, as my son, Harry, was born and I was adjusting to being a parent. At home I'd converted a double garage into a pool room, with a sofa, TV and a fruit machine. I had friends round regularly, but I also started running mini competitions that were well attended. We got 32 players in one night! So when Jen encouraged me to open a business I didn't have to be asked twice. I took over the old South Street Snooker Club and removed a few of the big tables to put the emphasis on pool. I recruited my good friend Lyndsey Roberts who came in to manage the club. She now plays for England Ladies. I also took on my nephew, Stu Gregory, who is now one of the best players in the region. Within a few months we attracted loads of county players and local teams who all wanted to play at the club. It didn't cost me a fortune to take the place on and I doubt it will make me rich, but it makes me happy and very proud that I've established a good club in the town that gave me a chance. I've made sure that the tables are a good standard, but getting the atmosphere right is also very important to players. We called it Dishers, because you dish the balls up when you break at the start of a game and go on to clear the table."

Although running a club had certain kudos, as well as bringing in money, the spin-off benefit was improved performances for the owner. This would take Dave to yet another level. "What I noticed most was that the extra pool practice was actually making me a much better player. I got my third England trial in March 2006 and, unlike other attempts in previous seasons, I qualified after a tense final round against a Humberside County player called Andy Lakin. I was on top of the world, playing with the most talented players in the country, representing England. All because of Dishers! Since then it's been a fantastic journey and all of the top players have visited our club on South Street. Recently we had Keith Brewer here and he's been at the top for 20 years. That was a real honour, and it brought back memories of a frame I was playing for England. All I could hear in the background was Keith shouting 'come on Preecey'. You just can't buy that…"

Dave with Keith Brewer.

Chris Turner
King for a Season

Watching the speedway stars race around Crewe's Earle Street track was fantastic, but at seventeen Chris Turner swapped the shale terrace for a Crewe Kings vest. He only enjoyed one season in Crewe colours riding with men he had idolised just a few years before, but that didn't stop him becoming a local hero himself...

"We lived on a farm on the edge of Warmingham, so Crewe was where we went shopping or sometimes out for a meal. Then dad took me to the very first speedway meeting at Earle Street in 1969, when I was eleven years old. I loved the whole experience from the start, and we only missed two home fixtures across those fantastic seasons. That was because we went on holiday. We'd gone to Abersoch and dad planned to drive back to catch the speedway, but my mum put her foot down and told us to stop being so daft! What I always loved about Crewe was the huge track. You got covered with shale, and as a kid that was all part of it. You could stand where you liked, right up against the fences or on the barriers. There wasn't much health and safety, but that added to the excitement. You just used common sense and kept clear of the bikes. The roar of engines was amazing and the closer you got the better. Hearing those machines was a big part of it for me, that and going home with a fine, red dust all over my hair and clothes. Mum went mad of course, and she always threw me in the bath!"

Most are content enjoying sports from the sidelines, but fate played its part when Chris entered his teenage years and he soon got much closer to his boyhood heroes. "Barry Meeks used to ride for Crewe and we got to know him down at the track. Most of the riders were friendly and he was always happy to chat. Then he bought a garage near us at the junction with Warmingham Lane. It's called Crewe Engines now, but it was also a petrol station years ago. As well as the speedway he was a grass track rider, so my first experiences on a bike were on the fields behind our farm, racing around with people like Barry, Jakey Jones from Crewe Works, Jeff Williams, Tony Ravenscroft and my best mate David Blackburn. It was serious stuff with meetings here, over in the Midlands, Lancashire and North Wales. There wasn't a league but you played for trophies and pride when riders got together. What I liked about the grass tracks was their similarity to speedway. They were both slippy and smooth, and that suited me."

The youngster (142) racing with Dave Blackburn.

With work on his dad's farm important to the family and riding taking more of his time, it was no surprise that Chris put school studies to one side. "I didn't go much in my final year, helping with jobs around the farm and practicing when I could. I also started doing bits of work for Terry Lowe who made the fibreglass parts for a lot of the speedway riders. There was no youth team at Crewe while I was riding the grass tracks, so I had to look elsewhere when I decided that I'd step up to the shale tracks. I got an opportunity at Belle Vue and I remember practicing across the winter of 1974 there, and occasionally at the Stoke circuit. People started to notice me and I think Barry might have put a word in here and there. I decided to sign for Belle Vue, but I wasn't quite good enough for the top division at the time. There was a chance to go on loan to Stoke, but Crewe came in for me just after the 1975 season had started. I jumped at the chance. Crewe was a fantastic track, one of the biggest. You had to buy a special engine sprocket, it was that big. Although I'd seen every inch of the circuit as a supporter, I'd not managed to practice there. They didn't have sessions for non-riders, probably because it cost money to open the place up. So I was terrified when I made my debut for 'The Kings' in April that year. I didn't want to make any mistakes. People were watching me!"

The nerves didn't last and in his first outing for Crewe he won his debut heat. "I had unbelievable butterflies, but I won that first race on adrenalin. A rookie beating established riders was an amazing feeling. I was on top of

Chris (far right) and Graham Drury in action versus Bradford in 1975.

the world. But it was a real team effort and the lads around me were fantastic. Graham Drury was the captain and he was a great influence. There was Stuart Cope alongside me, and the grass track lads all came to support me. They either helped to push the bikes off or they pitched in and raked the track at the end of each race. Mick Vaughan helped with my engines, while Jeff, Tony, Dave and Jakey all encouraged me from the pits. Stepping out in the leathers and wearing the Crewe Kings colours made me feel like a real pro."

Having good team mates was essential, especially when heats got lively. "Speedway can be tough out on the track but the riders are gentlemen when the heats finish. Some are more aggressive than others, but I don't remember anyone during my time trying to deliberately cause another rider to have an accident. Crashes always look dramatic but you're trained to fall off properly. I had a few tumbles but you usually got back on for the next heat. Supporters see riders sliding into each other but you're taught to drop your bike and not go over the top when a man's down on the track. If you did you'd probably hurt yourself just as much. It's like a code of conduct, respect for the other men. That's a well-known thing in speedway. You're competing hard to win races but I never met anyone who would go out to hurt someone else. Jack Millen showed me the basics and taught me how to fall safely. He'd jump out in front of you and force you off your bike. It was like a driving instructor teaching you how to do an emergency stop!"

A solid first season suggested that the new rider was destined for great things with his hometown club, but before the 1976 season had started there was devastating news. "When I heard that 'The Kings' had folded I was gutted. We didn't get involved on the money side, or bother about the politics. We just concentrated on the speedway. So it was a massive shock. I loved my time at Earle Street and I needed another season at Crewe to become a really decent rider. I was almost there, winning races but with plenty to learn. So losing the Crewe stadium was a heartbreaker for me, as a rider and supporter. I went on to enjoy success with Ellesmere Port and Edinburgh but I always missed my time at Crewe. No regrets, but being able to win something with 'The Kings' would have been wonderful. It just wasn't to be."

The Earle Street track was used for banger racing in subsequent years but the speedway was never forgotten. In early 2009 a book was published to commemorate the 1969-75 era, and this coincided with a reunion for riders and fans. "The get-together on High Street was amazing. Seeing men like John Jackson and Dave Morton was really special. It was good to meet them as a man, because when I raced I was still just a boy really. They had families and responsibilities and I must have seemed very young to them. So getting together over thirty years later was a dream come true. We talked on equal terms. The Crewe track was wonderful and it still gives me goose bumps thinking about it. That night brought it all flooding back."

Chris warming up his bike in the Earle Street pits.

Matt Owen
The Wonder of Crewe

As a kid Matt Owen looked up at Rail House as it cast a shadow over his beloved football club. Years later, having followed his team up and down the country, his passion for Crewe Alexandra is undiminished. Working life is a desk on the eleventh floor of that high-rise office block, now allowing him to keep tabs on things below…

"Growing up on Manor Way I was never far from 'The Alex'. The nearby cattle market off Barker Street was my playground, and along with my mates we'd all pretend that we were superstars. Of course, I was always an Alex player! We painted goalposts on a wall and spent hours playing football, often arguing whether the ball had hit the post. We also used to sneak onto the club's Astro pitch behind the old, wooden main stand. We couldn't afford to hire it; so playing on that flat surface with mini goals was like Wembley to us. My dad wasn't a football fanatic, so he only took me to the occasional Bank Holiday fixture. I wanted more than that and I was hooked from an early age. So I was always nagging friends and neighbours to take me with them. By the late '80s I was a regular at home matches, using my own pocket money to get in. I wasn't old enough to travel to away games, so I was devastated that I missed the promotion party at Tranmere at the end of that season."

Despite pressure from friends at school, there was only ever one team for Matt. "Other kids used to ask me which 'proper' club I supported. They couldn't understand that I was only interested in Crewe Alex. That changed when I got my first real taste of cup action, a game against the mighty Liverpool - home and away in the League Cup. I managed to secure tickets for both games and my mates were really jealous. It was the usual story, although they supported Liverpool or Man United, few of them had seen them live. What made it really special was going to a big match on a school night! It was a fantastic experience, seeing my favourite players take on internationals that I had only seen on TV before. My hero, Andy Sussex, put us 1-0 up that night and 'The Kop' was momentarily silenced. Although we lost the leg 5-1, I was incredibly proud to be an Alex fan. I didn't shed a tear that night, or when we were relegated or missed out on promotions over the following years. In fact, the only time I did was when a teacher told me that we'd sold Andy Sussex to Southend for £100,000. As far as I was concerned, he was priceless."

For most fans the bad times are, thankfully, tempered by the occasional promotion. For one schoolboy the good times started in May 1994, away at one of Crewe's local rivals. "My first proper experience of promotion was at Chester's Deva Stadium when we won on the last day. I just remember jumping up and down, delirious that we were going up. It felt that the club was really moving forward with Dario Gradi, who was already a respected manager. But the promotion season three years later took us to new heights, and it was a crazy time for me. I had my GCSE exams that year but my life revolved around the football, so I squeezed a bit of revision in when I could. The play-off semi-final at Luton stands out for me, mainly because of the fans. The noise was phenomenal and I remember how much it meant to the players. The way they celebrated after the goals and the scenes at the end of the game were amazing. Knowing that we were going to Wembley was the icing on the cake. Everything about that day in late May 1997 was special - on the supporters' coach, there and back on the day. It was hot, the build-up to the match was exciting and the game was tense, far too tense! We should have beaten Brentford by three or four goals, but we had to wait until the final whistle to know that a single strike from Shaun Smith was enough to take us to the second tier of English football. It didn't sink in for a while, even when we were back on Nantwich Road singing and dancing outside the pubs. The flags were waving and horns

Alex fans at Wembley, May 1997.

blasted up and down the busy street. It's those special moments that make it all worthwhile."

Observers of the game often talk about supporter loyalty, but this was sorely tested years later when Crewe Alexandra's long-serving manager stepped aside and allowed his apprentice to take control of the first team. "The Steve Holland era followed Dario's demise as a manager. We had a fantastic adventure in the higher division, for nearly ten years, but I suppose we all knew it had to end. It was the way we fell back down the leagues that disappointed supporters. I felt that Holland was pushed into the job and, as usual, the fans didn't have a say in matters. He was given a chance but he didn't win games. We'd had a bad run and with him in charge it looked as though we were going down again. So I was part of a very vocal protest that took place at the Alex and several away games leading up to his departure. The way the whole saga ended disappointed me, not because of our protests but the way the club's senior management conducted themselves. The process was drawn out over months. It should have been done sooner. In my opinion, they made Holland suffer. I was disappointed that he didn't succeed because he was a Crewe man. He played and coached here for years. But he often said in press conferences that it was a results game. So he failed. When we played Leyton Orient at home, his final game, I'd say that half of the crowd were against the manager. He had to go."

Changes happen at all football clubs, but for Matt the biggest disappointment has been what he sees as a growing divide between supporters and senior management. "It used to be a real family occasion at the Alex. There's still a good bunch of people who meet up, enjoy a few beers and some banter, and yet it doesn't feel the same. You don't get to meet as many players or club officials after the game and everything has become very formal. Promotion in 1997 was a fantastic achievement and we went on to build the new main stand, but the atmosphere disappeared. After that, I feel that we have stood still. Financial deals by some of the directors have left fans suspicious and I sometimes feel like an outsider. I'd like to see stability at the club again, as we had that for years. But I feel that the people running the club have lost touch. This is a community club but I no longer see it as a family club. Over the years it's hard to imagine the amount of miles that have been clocked up supporting Crewe Alexandra. Getting to games became a priority when I was a teenager, and so many things have been put to one side because of football. But I love the club. When my job with Atos Origin took me to the top of Rail House I was delighted. I can't stop myself taking a look down at the pitch each day, watching the ground staff and seeing if the games are going to be playable when it's cold and icy. I sometimes fall out with the players and people who run the club, but 'The Alex' will always be a part of my life…"

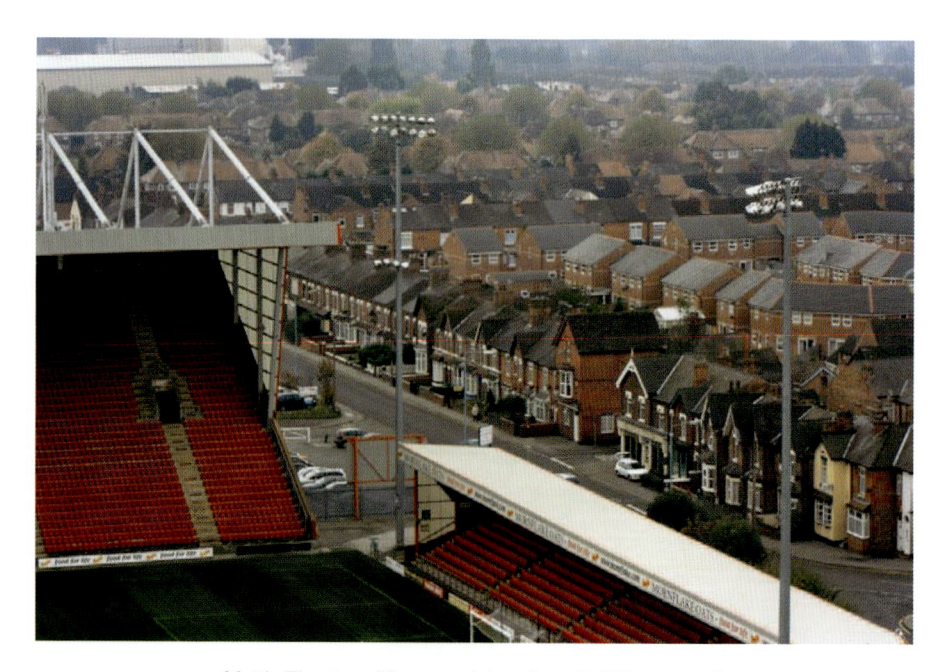

Matt's Theatre of Dreams, taken from Rail House roof.

David Cope
Mill Street Marbles

During the Second World War, German bombers failed to destroy the streets where David Cope grew up. However, successive post-war councils built high-rise blocks and demolished his Mill Street stomping ground. Still, the memories of a happy childhood can never be taken away...

"Wesley Street was a marvellous place to grow up. I was born just before war started, so my early childhood was dominated by shortages, air raid sirens and people making do with what they could get hold of. We didn't have much, but we enjoyed life. I had eight brothers and sisters, so there was never much spare to go around. We were a minute from the train station, near to some of the great railway workshops, there were pubs and shops on every corner and people were proud of their terraced homes. Steps were swept and windows were always kept clean. People were proud back then and there were no cars to worry about, just hundreds of bikes – especially when the men poured out of Crewe Works at tea time. We'd wave at some and wait for men we knew to cycle down our street. The school on Pedley Street was only a few yards away, and I still remember a lovely teacher called Mrs Cotton. She was strict but fun."

Post-war Crewe did its best to recover from bomb damage and the other economic effects of the conflict, while kids like David made the most of simple games. "We played marbles whenever we could, around the streets and anywhere there was a bit of space. In the mornings we'd head off to school and play along the gutters. They were great if you wanted a long stretch to roll them, as long as they weren't blocked up with leaves. So it was usually in the spring and summer. We had big black and white ones, about an inch wide, called 'stonkers'. We'd make a hole in the ground and put smaller marbles around it.

With friends on Wesley Street in 1952.

Then you'd flick the 'stonker' and see how many you could knock into the hole. I was pretty good. Marbles provided us with plenty of fun, easy to get hold of, just a few pennies when you had to buy them. Most of them were free, as you'd swap them or get them from older brothers and sisters. Another game we played used a piece of wood, like a cricket bat. It had holes dug into it at regular intervals, and we'd flick marbles down to see if we could get them in the holes. You scored different points depending where you landed, and you paid out in marbles. One day, in school, a lad put his hand up and said I'd got his glass eye. He was right, but I'd won it in a game. We found out that he regularly used it when we were playing marbles outside!"

Not all games were above board, but that added to the excitement. "Sometimes, when we had a few coins, we'd play pitch and toss down the alleys. Someone would stand lookout in case a policeman came past, the rest of us would flip coins against the wall to see who could win the most heads and tails. It was considered to be gambling, so if we got caught we'd be in trouble. They'd drag you home to your parents and you'd get a good clip round the ear, or worse. Something else we did, sometimes frowned upon if you were a kid, was to collect cigarette packets. Not for the ciggies, but the cards inside - and also the special wrappers on the packs. The cards would be pictures of wildlife, movie stars or footballers. Although I wasn't an Alex fan, I did sneak into the ground a few times. Most of the men who stood on

Demolition at the Nantwich Road/Mill Street junction.

the terraces smoked in those days, so after a match there were hundreds of packets on the floor. There was one wrapper I could never find for my collection, but one day when a couple of us crept into the ground I saw it. *Three Castles* was the brand, a really famous old name. I was delighted, and ran all the way home to tuck it safely away with my other packs. Getting the special ones made your friends really jealous, so collecting those packs was a great way to stand out even when you had money."

Like all active lads, football, fishing and messing about in water soon dominated any spare time, and the kids around Mill Street didn't have too far to travel. "We played football on the fields off Tommy's Lane, down by the fire station. We'd leave the house in the summer holidays at eight o'clock in the morning and not come back until it was dark. Loads of us played together, no money for sweets and often no food during the day. We'd take a bottle of water to keep us going. If it wasn't football, we'd be messing about in the brook, the River Waldron. We weren't bad lads, but we used to dam it up and play there for hours, diving in from the bridge. The Crewe Baths was open by then, but we couldn't afford to use that. So the brook was our bit of water. That's where some kids learned to swim. It wasn't very clean, though, and a few of my friends caught diseases, that later affected their feet and bones. Still, that didn't stop us mucking around. It was fun and free."

As he got older, David would stray further afield, and trips out with friends often involved lengthy expeditions. "We loved to go fishing, although we only had basic equipment. We'd use anything to make a rod, often a cheap cane from Harper's Ironmongers shop on Nantwich Road, and some cheap nylon for the line. The River Waldron ran past a large pool up at Crewe Hall, and the story was that during the war it was sabotaged to stop the Germans using its reflection to navigate at night. So the fish escaped into the brook and we fished sections out in the country, around the Mill Street Bridge and also by Crewe Baths. We caught some great roach and perch but always tossed them back. I did that as a young man, but you don't get many fish in the brook these days."

One form of entertainment came to Crewe once, sometimes twice each year. Although expensive, when the circus arrived there was an opportunity to see a show for nothing. "The animals and entertainers were great. They used to send the elephants up on the train, walk them up from the station and stable them behind the Royal Hotel. We'd sneak in and take a look, as we could hear them from our house. They'd march them down through town to perform at the Lyceum Theatre. Sometimes, to publicise the shows, they'd have a parade through town. They had all sorts on show, and they'd give us a free ticket if we'd walk with a horse or donkey for a few hours. When I was about 16, I remember the kangaroo they had performing. It had boxing gloves and they'd let you have a minute in the ring with it, to try your luck. It was huge and it punched and punched without stopping. You had no chance. It was a laugh and we chat about it for ages talking about the time we got floored by a kangaroo!"

They were hard times but David wouldn't swap them for anything on offer today. "I often think that kids today have got everything, and yet they have nothing. We had a wonderful time around Mill Street in the 1940s and 50s, and it breaks my heart that most of it was pulled down. There's not much community left these days. Memories always stay with you, and I was the marble champion. They can knock down buildings, but they can't take away my childhood crown!"

One of the remaining buildings during demolition around Mill Street.

Peter Ollerhead
Grumpy Old Men

Cars, Christianity and the history of Crewe have dominated Peter Ollerhead's life since his family returned to the town as World War Two began. Later years have seen books sold at the town's only remaining independent shop, many personal projects published, and all of them discussed with the help of a few grumpy old friends…

"My father grew up here, started in Crewe Works, but then got a job in Manchester at the Ford car plant. He met my mother, married, and then relocated to the Dagenham factory down south. So I was born in Essex in 1937, but when the war started my mother didn't want me evacuated to the countryside with other kids. Luckily, my grandfather wrote to my father and told him about the new aero engine factory in Crewe, that he called 'Rose Rice'. Mum wasn't keen as she thought it was an old girlfriend of his, but that was just how my grandfather pronounced it! So we moved to Crewe and eventually settled on Smith Grove in 1939 when the council started to develop the West End estates. Perhaps my earliest childhood memory is of King George VI and his visit to Royce's in 1940. I recall a lot of fuss, but it was my father's tale about the King wearing make-up as he walked around the factory that always stayed with me."

That visit was the spark that ignited a young boy's love of cars from an early age. "The estate was new when we moved in, so it was full of young families. The war ended and we had plenty of open space to explore around Minshull New Road and Pyms Lane. We'd often go down to the tip area and play on the sandy banks that existed back then. As kids we didn't notice the shortages too much, as your parents would always make sure that you had enough while they would sometimes go without. I remember my sister being told off once, for putting too much jam on her bread! There were few sweets, but you didn't miss what you didn't have. Cars were a real luxury item, and our family was lucky enough to be one of the first on the street to own one. It was a real adventure going for a ride in a car, and I always looked forward to getting my own. I managed that early in my working life, when I joined my father and got a job at Royce's three weeks after my fifteenth birthday in 1952. I borrowed some money from my mother, and paid £75 for a Morris 10/4 from a superintendent at the factory who fixed up cars at work. He even gave them a job number! In those days, nobody left cars parked on the road. They were always stored in garages or carports at night. I had a space at a communal garage on Glover Street, along with several other people. Sometimes, you had to push other cars out to get to your own! After that I moved it to Count Bartelli's garage, near Merrill's Bridge on West Street. For a few shillings each month you could park, under cover, behind the garage showroom. The Count was a famous masked wrestler, a decent chap called Geoff Condliffe who was unbeaten for twenty years. The garage was a sideline to supplement the money he won in the ring. He was eventually beaten and was forced to remove his mask, but he went on to own a chain of hugely successful garages."

Still based in the West End, local youth work at the Glover Street Chapel would provide a varied social life and an introduction to a special lady. "There was a lot of Christian work done with the kids, sports days and trips out to the country. We'd often walk for miles, over to Whitchurch and Beeston, have a picnic and then return home worn out. We weren't out to preach to the youngsters, but it was a good way to introduce them to a Christian way of life. Occasionally, a number of Crewe churches met up through the Youth For Christ movement, and it was at one of these events, at the old

Glover Street garage.

Corn Exchange, that I met my wife. She was based on Gresty Road, working at the Railway Mission that stood at the junction with Nantwich Road. It was built in 1909, one of varied places of worship demanded by the diverse population that arrived because of the railway. In fact, at one time, Crewe had as many non-conformist churches as Sheffield – a city seven times the size of Crewe! A wedding licence was granted so that we could marry at the mission – and we were the first couple to do so at that site. Then, a year later, one of our bridesmaids did the same. The latter was memorable for their wedding and because the old church was pulled down the next day. It's where Rail House was built to give the network a regional office block. The Railway Mission moved further down Gresty Road, before returning to the corner of Hewitt Street. So we made our own little piece of history."

The town's religious diversity is something that has always fascinated Peter, and a subject that he would study at college in later life. "There was a chap called Frank Kettell who lived on Ruskin Road. He'd been involved with several churches, including the old chapel on Underwood Lane that is set back from the road and recently became a bookmaker's. That was once controlled by a breakaway group of the Plymouth Brethren, and Frank was part of the congregation. When he married a wealthy lady, he came into some money and built his own church – the Glover Street Chapel, opened in the early 1930s. So I had always known him through church, and my mother used to clean at his house. When his wife died he eventually moved to a

The last service at the Railway Mission.

retirement home. I chatted to him over the years and he always had a story to tell me, often revealing details about the many churches dotted around the town. When he died he donated the chapel to the church group, helping to preserve another piece of Crewe. He also gave me a lot of photos and historical papers, and that ignited my interest in local history. I'd been thinking about my future, and over one summer I completed a few 'O' levels. With some formal qualifications I had options, so in 1966 I decided to leave Rolls-Royce and started a new adventure in the teaching profession."

Following Frank Kettell's generosity, a serious interest in second hand books started, and with it a love of research that also led to Peter putting pen to paper. "My collection grew quickly as I bought up large lots of books from dealers, markets and auctions. I'd keep the ones I wanted and sell the rest.

So the hobby paid for itself and encouraged me to set up the Copnal Books business on Meredith Street. Between 1972 and 1975, I completed my masters degree thesis on non-conformist churches. That was over 100,000 words and it ensured that no written project would ever seem daunting again! Still, it was the Crewe story that always fascinated me. I was lucky enough to meet men like W. H. Chaloner, who covered every inch of the town's history with a fine toothcomb and wrote extensively about Crewe's early development. His enthusiasm, dry sense of humour and passion spurred me on and, when I finally retired from teaching in the late 1990s, I was able to progress a number of written projects myself. This town has a fabulous tale to tell, mainly because of the flow of people it has enjoyed for nearly two centuries. These days, the Grumpy Old Men's Club at the shop on Friday mornings is a great source of information. It's somewhere that old friends, customers and the occasional stranger can meet, chat, swap tales and remember how things were. There's usually a disagreement about something, a squabble over names or dates, but it's always light-hearted. Actually selling books tends to get in the way…"

The 'grumpy old men' - Billy Consterdine, Peter, Harry Jones and Brian Edge.

Albert Dean
Voice of the Airwaves

Spinning discs at private parties was Albert Dean's passion during his teenage years, but some fatherly advice encouraged him to run a trendy clothing shop that would become the place to be in the heart of Crewe. However, it wasn't too long before he was once again holding a microphone and commanding the airwaves…

"My early school life was spent on West Street - at the infant and then junior schools. I had some happy years at both, with a teacher called Mr Appleton a major influence as he encouraged my interest in mathematics. It certainly gave me a head for business in later life. Before that, while I was still at senior school, I teamed up with some friends at the St. Barnabas youth club hall and started a mobile disco. We had some brilliant years playing at weddings and private functions and I thought it might become my career. Unfortunately, the DJ work got in the way of 'A' level studies and my dad wasn't impressed. He said that music would spoil my life, just as football had ruined his!"

Unlike many rebellious teenagers Albert took parental advice and realised that discos were unlikely to make his fortune. So, soon after leaving school, he sold his decks and speakers to a friend and formed a family partnership. "My dad and I opened a clothes shop in 1976. It was known as *Posters Boutique* on lower Market Street, and was later simplified to just *Posters*. I invested some of the cash I'd recouped from the sale of disco kit so that we could increase the range of stock. We sold all kinds of menswear, from suits to flashy tracksuits that were fashionable in the late 1970s. The business boomed so we soon looked for bigger premises. We found a great unit by Tony's Chippy, across the road from The Grand Junction pub. The only downside was that we were near to a number of the town centre pubs. The windows were often smashed over the weekend, and it was worst during the World Cup of 1978. Otherwise, it was a decent shop. Moody's the jewellers owned it and the rent and rates were reasonable. However, in 1979 there were massive changes to the area. The West Street extension meant that, after much controversy, The Chetwode Arms disappeared, and part of the Market Street shopping area was bulldozed - including our first shop. We were settled by then, but we discovered that there were also plans to redevelop the area around our business. So, when they announced that the Market Centre as we know it today would be built, we were forced to move shops again."

Luckily, the unit next to Greenwoods on Victoria Street was vacant and was the perfect spot for the increasingly popular shop. "That move put us right in the centre of town, increased our footfall and took the takings to the highest levels since we started the business. That was fortunate, because the costs were phenomenal. It was a fantastic time for fashion and we started selling the best lines for young men. We sold stretch jeans before anyone else and pushed into the leisurewear, with big names like Ennesse on the racks. Then Woolworth's closed down and that was the beginning of the end for me. They broke up the once huge shop that connected Market Street with Queensway, creating a number of smaller units. Because of our success and reputation in the area, a *Top Man* opened and was closely followed by *Concept Man*. That was later known as *River Island*. So the competition was fierce and we did well to hold our own for a couple of years."

The successful business was also a great hang out and renowned for its music. "It was more a meeting place in the end, although our customers all spent plenty of money there. The shop was my real education; a proper eye opener to what life in Crewe was really like. I

Posters staff in the 1980s.

suppose I missed the DJ work so there was always a music system blasting out the latest tunes. We had a superb deal with the nearby Virgin music store that gave us the latest chart releases to play, providing that we recommended them to our customers. I even put a jukebox in the window one Christmas, and towards the late 1980s there were music videos playing as customers browsed. We always liked to be first! If I hadn't been a clothes shop owner I'd have been a record dealer, but you can't look back. The shop was a great experience and some bizarre characters came through the door. One day, around 1989, I gave some flared trousers to a trendy, young band that were trying to make it in the music industry. It was old stock and I was just doing them a favour, as they seemed a decent bunch of lads from Northwich. I didn't know then, but they went on to great success. They called themselves

The Charlatans! Nothing lasts forever, and in 1990 the business was sold when I decided to return to education and started a degree in Business and Accounting. I soon realised that this was the route I wanted to take, as I'd always loved working with numbers. I eventually became a college lecturer in Newcastle-under-Lyme. As it happened, the shop didn't last much longer either. A combination of the rival clothes shops and the early 90s recession hit them hard. So I was fortunate, more through luck than judgement."

Music, however, was always a part of his social life, so when a former employee from *Posters* mentioned a new venture he was quick to sign up. "In the summer of 1994, when I'd finished my college course, a mate called Mike McHugh told me about a guy called Harry Nelson who was starting a Crewe radio station. He was looking for people to get involved. During the 80s we ran a quiz team under the shop's banner, called *The Posters Pop Squad*. That was with Mike, Andy Scoffin and Paul Morris. Then, between 1985 and 1987, I went on to present *The Posters Pop Challenge* with Andy, a regular quiz event at The Hunters Lodge. It was packed out every Sunday night. So we had all been involved in presenting before and had the experience and knowledge a local station needed. That first attempt was called YFM and I cringe when I listen to my first broadcast. I was nervous and, typically, I tried to put too much into the show."

Albert and Andy Scoffin.

The first broadcasts came from a small studio at South Cheshire College, off Dank Bank Avenue, with two temporary licences giving wannabe DJs a chance to hit the airwaves. "YFM was a decent project but didn't progress. Witch FM was the next incarnation and broadcast from Imperial Chambers on Prince Albert Street in 1999. Both attempts at local radio deserved more support, but there were pieces of the jigsaw missing each time. Then, in 2008, The Cat FM finally happened. A number of like-minded people pulled together and the M Club on High Street offered us free space for a studio. Everything was more structured and organised, with a dedicated fundraiser bringing in the cash required to drive the initiative forward. Three successful broadcasts later and there are high hopes that The Cat will secure a permanent licence. The Crewe & Nantwich Community Radio Society has been formed and I think that we have a much greater chance of success. There's even an online presence when we're not on the air, so that's fantastic progress. The area needs its own radio station, and fingers crossed that it will finally happen in 2010. I love being involved behind the microphone, just as I was in my teenage years. Long may it continue…"

Albert in The Cat's M Club studio, September 2008.

Joey Singleton
Punches and Pints

Working hard in boxing gyms from the age of eight, always on top of his game, Joey "The Jab" Singleton was a winner in the ring. Ultimately denied a shot at the world title, he managed pubs and a security business before concentrating on training the Crewe boxers of the future...

"There wasn't much equipment when I started out. I joined my brothers, Tommy and Billy, who were at a school gym in Norris Green, Liverpool. When that place closed down, we went over to Fazakerley, near Kirby. It was an old RAF camp, rock bottom basic, and we had to pump up the oil lamps and light fires to keep warm while we trained in the winter. There were some good people, though, and they taught me some valuable lessons. That gym turned out some great fighters, like John Conteh, Azumah Nelson, Shea Neary and Paul Hodkinson. I started sparring with a guy named John Lloyd. He was bigger and older than me, so I had to work hard. That made me determined, and it made me the fighter I am today. I won the schoolboy championships from eleven years of age, and then became junior champion at fifteen. Turning pro was never daunting, because I had great confidence in my ability. There were forty professional fights across my career before I retired at 32 years of age. I'd been in the ring for 24 years, so the body was getting tired. I had some great wins and won the British Welterweight title faster than anyone else. After eleven fights I held the Lonsdale Belt. So I achieved a lot but saw myself as a failure because I didn't fight for the World Title."

While training still dominated his life, Joey also took a pub, The Red Cow, in Peckham High Street, in south London. That gave him a taste for business life after boxing, and the licensed trade would ultimately pay the bills. "The London pub was hectic and I ran that with a business partner. We eventually came back to Merseyside and did well, but we wanted something a little bigger. That's what brought me to Crewe, and we settled on the Bear's Paw in Warmingham. We bought that for £250,000 in 1987 and had some great times, offering good food and entertainment. That lasted six years but we realised that it wouldn't make our fortune. It was too far out of town, and on foggy, winter nights we'd close the place because the bar was empty. I needed a pub with regular trade, part of a busy scene and with proper drinkers. That's what I knew best. So we sold up."

The Brunswick on Nantwich Road would eventually provide the bustling pub environment Joey craved, but another business opportunity arose that would establish him as one of the best-known faces in town. "I started doing the pub doors in Sandbach, but I realised that there was a need for a proper firm in Crewe. If the police, drinkers and other pubs are confident about the door staff, then you can have a well-run operation. So I formed Lonsdale Security in 1994 and it grew quickly, with nearly 100 staff working the pub doors one Christmas! I'd run the door at Clancy's for a while, and I was told that Nantwich Road felt safe, and that people trusted my team. At one time that stretch was like Blackpool's Golden Mile, busy pubs everywhere and people having a good time. There were a few rogues, but you can handle them in Crewe. I've lived in Liverpool and London and some of the locals here wouldn't stand a chance in the big cities. On football days we had a few handy lads down from the big city clubs. That happened in the Royal Hotel one night when Manchester United visited. Glasses were smashed and one of the fruit machines was emptied. I knew one of their fans, a Crewe lad, and I told him that I wanted all fifty of them out. The bar didn't want their money. He said it might kick off, but because he trusted me and respected that I was head doorman, he got them to leave – no fuss. I even told the police to keep an eye on them as they went to other pubs along the street, but they came to say goodbye and shake my hand after the match. It's a rough game and you have plenty of problems, but I was well respected. You have to deal with

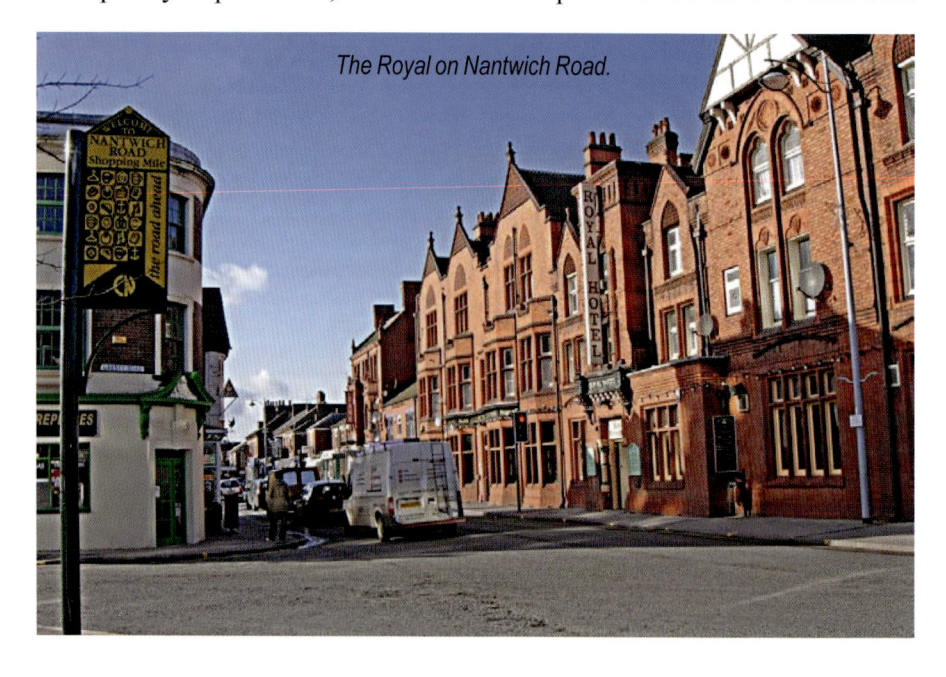

The Royal on Nantwich Road.

Photo by Simon J. Newbury.

certain people when trouble starts, and no matter what you say they'll have a grudge against you. So over the years I had fifteen death threats. I can live with that, but it's not acceptable when people start intimidating people who are close to you. My partner has been put through too much, so when a couple of national firms started putting door teams in the area I knew that was a good time to call it a day."

In the background, Joey's passion for boxing continued when he established the Crewe ABC, giving youngsters somewhere to train and learn the ropes. "The first gym was set up at the Greystone Park youth club, and we got by with some basic bits of equipment. For a while I doubled-up with a lad who taught kickboxing, but I wanted more control and to offer the best training to the kids. So we went solo and started to build something special. We spent a few years at the Macon House complex, by The Lollipop Club, but that wasn't big enough as we started to expand. So we settled at the old Camm Street gym, and they gave us a massive space that was perfect. There are forty to fifty fighters there some nights, and the council have been really supportive helping us get grants for extra training gear. We took the best of the fighters all over the area competing against other clubs and I was amazed how quickly some of the kids progressed. It's all about listening to your coach, because if you carry on thinking that you know it all you'll end up on your back. I've got some great lads at the gym and they want to learn. I've watched them improve and it's been great passing on my experience."

Finally, in early 2008, amateur boxing was brought back to Crewe. "I felt so proud that I could stage bouts in the town. It meant a lot to our fighters, not having to travel all the time. They stand up and fight in front of a home crowd and it makes all the difference. You see them walking tall, looking like they have gained an inch and a few years of experience. So whether we break even or make a few quid for the club, it's worth performing in front of their friends and family. It helps their development. The main function room at Crewe Alexandra's ground is a fantastic venue, plenty of seating, a big bar and they let us use the club's changing rooms. It's got a huge car park and it's close to the train station as well. So we've built up a good relationship with the football club and I'm hoping we can carry on holding events there in the future. Fighters like Alfie Sackey have a real chance, and he is always learning. He's been fighting for the England team and, because he listens to me, I think he's got a great chance in the heavyweight division. He'll need a lucky break or two, maybe something that I didn't get, but he'll succeed if he keeps training hard. I've always felt that I should have been given a crack at the world title, so now my ambition is to train one of my own kids. It will happen one day..."

Joey with Lee Murray (left) and Alfie Sackey.

Images of Modern Day Crewe

Queens Park lodges by the main gates. A project to restore the park's grounds to former Victorian glories commenced in 2006 and is due to be completed in 2011. The lodges will be refurbished, whilst all other structures will be replaced.

Tea and cakes at one of Wulvern Housing's open days on Crewe's Derby Docks estate. The social housing provider manages over 5,500 homes across Crewe and Nantwich, including several larger facilities for elderly residents.

Alex fans at Dishers Pool Club on South Street, enjoying a pint before a home game at the Alexandra Stadium. Over the years the venue has been both snooker hall and a nightclub, until local lad and England international Dave Preece focused on the growing pool scene.

The Edleston Road School, seen from the junction with Stalbridge Road. The pupils moved to Gainsborough Road School in 2008 and the building is now used as additional office space for staff from South Cheshire College.

Market Square before refurbishment in the summer of 2009, although the Britannia War Memorial was moved to Municipal Square in 2006. A plan to replace the old Queensway block and Big Bill clock tower with a new shopping complex is planned for 2012.

The Crewe Labour Group launching the party's manifesto outside the offices of Gwyneth Dunwoody in April 2008. Soon after, the long-standing MP passed away and the town was the focus of national media.

Enjoying a laugh as another pint is served at The British Lion on Nantwich Road. Affectionately known as "The Pig", the much-loved pub has prospered as others have closed. The staff, friendly customers and cosy atmosphere have all contributed to its success.

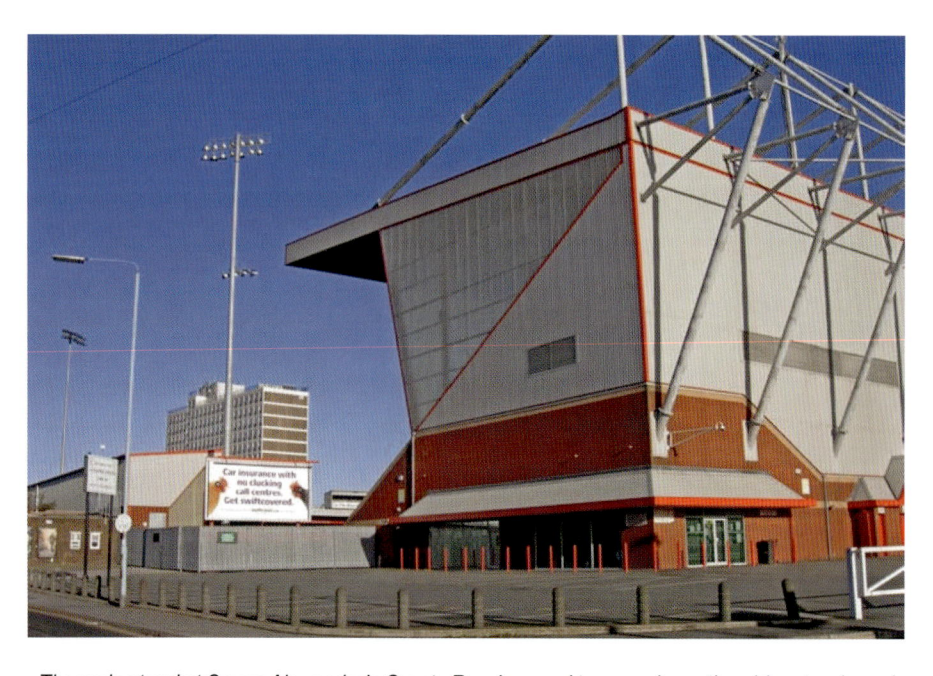

The main stand at Crewe Alexandra's Gresty Road ground towers above the older stands and challenges nearby Rail House on the Crewe skyline. Built in 1999, the all-seat structure took the club's capacity above 10,000 for the first time in years.

New Housing on the corner of Ludford Street and Badger Avenue, built on land that was formerly part of the Ludford Street School complex. A tranquil outlook, the apartments look out across the beautiful grounds of Crewe Cemetery.

Having a laugh and a joke at Crewe Carnival on the main exhibition field in 2008. By the summer of 2009 work on Queens Park had progressed such that the town's annual carnival moved to the King George V playing fields.

Local MP Edward Timpson joins Crewe and Nantwich Mayor Brian Silvester, Mayoress Sheila Davies and officers from The Mercian Regiment (Cheshire) at the opening of a new Army recruitment office on Market Street in November 2008.

Webb Orphanage, known as Webb House, stands off Victoria Avenue near Queens Park. Chief Mechanical Engineer Francis Webb was the main benefactor, and the beautiful building was opened in 1912. In the 1970s and 80s it was used as a British Rail training centre.

The Phoenix Leisure Park offers bowling, cinema and bingo just a stone's throw from the town centre. Built on former railway land, the nearby cottages off Chester Street survived a fire that destroyed the General Offices.

Strike action on Pyms Lane at the council depot. UNISON members spoke to employees and visitors as discussions about pay and conditions were conducted at a national level. The depot faces Bentley Motors, and many of the car plant's workforce offered support.

Crewe councillor Roy Cartlidge in Market Square with the Dr Bike team that regularly visits the town. Advice, help and practical training was offered to cyclists as the public was encouraged to live a healthier lifestyle and, where possible, to go green.

A view of Earle Street shops in the town centre, seen from the corner of Municipal Square. Many of the shops have changed since this picture was taken, with the pub becoming Oscars in 2008. It was also known as the Cheese Hall and the Three Lamps.

A view of the Christ Church bell tower at sunrise, as seen from the Chester Bridge. The church is still used despite losing its roof in the 1980s, and there are big plans to make one of the railway company's earliest buildings a key part of town centre life in the future.

Flying the flag along West Street during the annual Crewe Carnival. Numbers have dropped over the years, and participation in the parade is not what it used to be. However, thousands still enjoy the splash of colour every August.

Firemen from Crewe entertaining the Christmas shoppers outside ASDA supermarket with a few well-known carols. Not necessarily the best singers in town, but a great effort on behalf of local charities.

Jubilee Garden in Hightown. A project to transform the gardens was completed in 2006 and it now offers a peaceful place to sit and walk. Originally opened to the public in 1927, the gardens celebrated the golden jubilee of the Borough of Crewe, formed in 1877.

Another busy day on Nantwich Road. Many of the original buildings still stand, dominated these days by solicitors offices on the right and specialist businesses on the left. Rail House has dominated the skyline for nearly half a century.

The Crewe branch of the Communication Workers Union are joined by colleagues from around the country to protest at plans to close the Crewe sorting office on Weston Road. The rally converged on Municipal Square to listen to speeches from union officials.

Characters entertaining the shoppers in Market Square, another event organised by the town centre management team. Events are staged to encourage shoppers to visit more often and spend longer in and around the town's shops, cafés and attractions.

St. Michael's Church in Coppenhall, as see from the Ford Lane entrance. A beautiful church that sits alongside its cemetery, shaded by giant horse chestnut trees. It was originally a wooden structure dating back to the 1300s, but the current red-brick structure was built in the 1880s.

College Gate housing development emerged as part of the transformation of land behind the old Ursuline Convent on Nantwich Road. The main building became a police training centre, and its grounds used for officers' accommodation.

Chaotic scenes in May 2008 when Conservative Edward Timpson won the Crewe and Nantwich by-election, taking a previously safe Labour seat. The new MP was joined by Tory leader David Cameron as he made his first speech in front of local people and national media.

Young rock band Sgt Wolfbanger on stage at The Box, a music venue on Pedley Street near Nantwich Road. The venue joined other pubs and clubs to establish the town's first widespread music festival called Crewe Live 08.

Clean lines, fresh paint and refurbished buildings on platform 12. The first phase of works to transform Crewe Station started in 2007, but many are disappointed that a complete overhaul was shelved because Network Rail started to investigate other track and signalling options.

Cheshire East's first mayor councillor Margaret Simon joins kids on Crewe's Derby Docks to celebrate Worlds Alive Day in July 2009. Many cultures came together, exchanging stories, sports and games, plus a variety of cooked dishes.

Red Nose Day at South Cheshire College is regularly celebrated by staff and students. The college will see its new campus completed in 2010, a tricky project that is being built alongside the existing tower off Dane Bank Avenue.

The band of the Kings Division lead the 1st Battalion the Mercian Regiment (Cheshire) along Queensway on a misty November morning in 2008. Despite the conditions a large crowd gathered along the route to welcome the bandsmen.

Mercian Regiment (Cheshire) soldiers march from Christ Church along Chester Street to celebrate their links to the area. The regiment was also accepting the freedom of the Borough of Crewe and Nantwich. Emotional friends and family lined the route.

A night time image from the roof of Rail House, looking down to Nantwich Road. The late night drinkers have long gone, the restaurants and takeaways have closed, and just a few cars can be seen heading home in the early hours.

Crewe Cemetery, opened in 1872, seen here in early autumn as the leaves have started to fall. As the town expanded over the next century it was obvious that space was an issue, and a new cemetery called Meadow Brook was opened off Minshull New Road in 2009.

The Couzens building at MMU Cheshire campus is part of the original site built around 1912 that served as a teacher training college. Now part of the Manchester Metropolitan University, student numbers total nearly 6000 and the campus is undergoing extensive expansion.

The losing Labour candidate in the 2008 Crewe and Nantwich by-election, Tamsin Dunwoody, was supported by many high-profile Labour ministers. Seen here with Jack Straw who literally got on his soap box and spoke to voters on Victoria Street.

Gresty Road End drummer Gary Blease keeps the rhythm going. A number of drums have featured at the ground over the years, and some fans will recall the trumpeter who entertained the crowds from the Popside in the 1990s.

Another aerial view of Crewe town centre, this time from the roof of the Delamere House council offices. Queensway and the Big Bill clock tower are to the left, with the BT building on Queen Street in the distance. Railway cottages off Chester Street can be seen to the right.

Crewe and Nantwich MP Edward Timpson was a relative unknown when the campaign teams took to the streets in May 2008. His family run Timpson's shoe repair shops, and he worked for many years as a Family Law Barrister at Crewe Law Courts.

The BMX track at Tipkinder by Queens Park received a much-needed transformation in 2008 and was later renamed the Shanaze Reade BMX Track in honour of the town's best known rider. A local lad is seen here showing off some aerial skills.